WINTER CABIN COOKING

WINTER CABIN COOKING

Dumplings, fondue, strudel, glühwein and other fireside feasts

LIZZIE KAMENETZKY

Photography by
NASSIMA ROTHACKER

RYLAND PETERS & SMALL
LONDON • NEW YORK

Senior Designer Toni Kay
Editor Kate Eddison
Production Mai-Ling Collyer
Art Director Leslie Harrington
Editorial Director Julia Charles
Publisher Cindy Richards

Prop Stylist Polly Webb-Wilson
Food Stylist Lizzie Kamenetzky
Indexer Vanessa Bird

First published in 2015 by
Ryland Peters & Small
20–21 Jockey's Fields
London WC1R 4BW
and
341 E 116th St
New York NY 10029

www.rylandpeters.com

Text © Lizzie Kamenetzky
Design and photographs
© Ryland Peters & Small 2015

ISBN: 978-1-84975-660-0

10 9 8 7 6 5 4 3 2 1

A CIP record for this book is available
from the British Library.

US Library of Congress CIP data has
been applied for.

Printed and bound in China

Notes

- Both British (Metric) and American (Imperial plus US cups) measurements are included in these recipes for your convenience, however it is important to work with one set of measurements and not alternate between the two within a recipe.
- All spoon measurements are level unless otherwise stated.
- Eggs are medium (UK) or large (US) unless otherwise specified. Uncooked or partly cooked eggs should not be served to the very old, the frail, young children, pregnant women or those with compromised immune systems.
- When a recipe calls for the grated zest of citrus fruit, buy unwaxed fruit and wash well before using. If you can only find treated fruit, scrub well in warm soapy water before using.
- Ovens should be preheated to the specified temperatures. We recommend using an oven thermometer. If using a fan-assisted oven, adjust temperatures according to the manufacturer's instructions.

CONTENTS

INTRODUCTION

MOUNTAINS ARE A PLACE OF MAGIC. From the smallest Cairngorm to the highest Rocky or Himalaya, there is something that draws you in, and up. I love the way you feel so small in the mountains, their untameable peaks watching over you from above. Breathing in that clear, crisp mountain air, just thinking about it makes me ravenously hungry.

The pace of mountain life is something that we should all embrace from time to time. We move so fast through our lives, always rushing, never enough time to cook, to eat, to enjoy, but in the mountains, life slows down. You can't get anywhere fast in the mountains, so you might as well relax and let it wash over you. These are places of long, schnapps-filled lunches and relaxed, laid back dinners with friends and family as the snow falls quietly around and time ceases to matter.

I've been lucky enough to grow up spending many happy holidays in the mountains and confess to being completely besotted with the way of life there, but more than anything I love the food. It is real, honest food that I want to get stuck into with both hands. In many ways unchanged for years. The emphasis is on local produce, with each region of the mountains having its specialities of which it is inordinately proud.

Winter is a particularly amazing time in any mountain range, and it is this winter fare that this book celebrates. Hearty food for cold days, full of flavour and warmth.

I learned to ski from a young age. My childhood vacations were not spent in the big Alpine resorts (although in later years I have visited and skied in many of them, and grown to love them in their own way), instead my parents chose to spend our breaks in a small and beautiful village, nestled in the Swiss Alps in the shadow of Mont Dolon and the Grand St Bernard Pass. When I am there, I can imagine the monks in centuries past, on their fur-lined skis, climbing the passes to their lofty monasteries, offering welcome sanctuary and simple repast to travellers and pilgrims coming in from the snow.

As the snow falls and covers the trees and cabins, a hush falls over the mountains. I could stand for hours just watching and listening to the snow fall, the way it makes everything so quiet that your ears somehow ring with the absence of sound. Even better is watching the snow from inside a cosy cabin, with a fire crackling and a steaming bowl of hot chocolate to warm you.

The mountains of Central Europe are famous for their variety of traditional dishes beloved by skiers and non-skiers alike. The food has developed over the centuries, influenced by the countries that make up its whole.

There are the Western Alps of Slovenia and Austria (the Tyrol) with their rich stews, noodles and dumplings. Further to the East you have Switzerland, France, Germany and Liechtenstein, famous for Savoie cheeses, rustic breads, schnitzels and sausages. In the South are Italy and Monaco, full of warming ragùs, polenta and gnocchi. Where the borders of these countries meet, the most wonderful fusion of flavours and traditions mingle to create some truly spectacular and memorable dishes for which the region as a whole has become famous.

Skiing is not just part of European culture, however, and, as a vacation, it has taken off around the world. The skiing food culture in the US and Canada has taken much of its influence from the mountain regions of Europe, but with their own twists and the additions of various celebrated national dishes.

Even if you don't enjoy throwing yourself down a frozen mountain on little wooden planks, you cannot fail to fall in love with the simplicity and deliciousness of the food of the mountains. The romanticism of the traditional ski chalet, of coming in from the cold air with rosy cheeks to be greeted by the amazing warmth and aroma of a hearty supper. This is food for warming the soul, for snuggling up against the cold chill outside. For firesides and crackling logs, blankets and slippers.

If you love the mountains, wherever you are from, then this book will inspire, delight and encourage you to bring these wonderful dishes into your own kitchen.

DUMPLINGS AND NOODLES

SCHLUTZKRAPFEN

These tasty little slippery parcels are similar to Polish pierogi and are traditionally filled with a classic mixture of spinach and ricotta. The rye pasta is silky and smooth and freezes brilliantly, so if you only want to make a few you can keep the rest for another time.

400 g/14 oz. spinach or chard
2 tablespoons olive oil
1 banana shallot, finely chopped
1 garlic clove, crushed
100 g/scant ½ cup ricotta cheese
25 g/scant ⅓ cup Parmesan, grated
freshly grated nutmeg
a small bunch of fresh chives, chopped
30 g/2 tablespoons unsalted butter
1 tablespoon walnut oil
sea salt and ground black pepper

FOR THE PASTA
175 g/heaping 1½ cups rye flour
75 g/½ cup 00 flour
1 egg
1 tablespoons olive oil
7 tablespoons water

MAKES 60 SMALL DUMPLINGS

Start by making the pasta. Mix the flours together with a generous pinch of salt. Make a well in the centre and add the egg, olive oil and water. Mix together with your fingers to form a soft pliable dough. Knead until smooth and supple and then wrap in clingfilm/plastic wrap and rest for 30 minutes.

Blanch the spinach or chard in boiling water for 1 minute then drain and refresh under cold water. Use your hands to squeeze out as much water as you can, then finely chop. Heat the oil in a pan and gently fry the shallot for 5 minutes, then add the garlic and cook for a further minute. Add to the bowl with the spinach or chard, and then add the ricotta, half the Parmesan, a good grating of nutmeg and half the chives. Mix well and season with plenty of salt and black pepper.

Roll out the dough as thinly as possible, you shouldn't need extra flour on your surface but if it sticks a little you could add a dusting. You could use a pasta maker if you have one to get it super thin but I like the rustic approach of hand rolling. Use a 7.5 cm/3 in. round pastry/cookie cutter to cut out discs of the dough, re-rolling the trimmings to get as many as possible. You should have about 60 discs.

Put a spoonful of the mixture into the centre of each disc. Dampen around the edge and fold over and press to seal so you have little half-moons. As you get used to making them, you can try to crimp the edges, but this is just for look and can be a bit fiddly, so start by just sealing them with straight edges.

Bring a pan of salted water to the boil, plunge the dumplings into it and cook for 2–3 minutes. Heat a large frying pan/skillet with the butter and walnut oil. Remove the cooked dumplings from the water with a slotted spoon and transfer straight to the buttery pan. The residual water from the dumplings with emulsify with the butter and oil to form a lovely glossy sauce. Scoop onto warm plates, then sprinkle with remaining Parmesan, scatter with the rest of the chives and serve.

FLEISCH KNÖDEL

2 tablespoons olive oil

1 onion, finely chopped

500 g/1lb. 2oz. mixed cooked and cured meats, such as leftover roast pork, lamb or chicken, cooked sausages or salami

freshly grated nutmeg

a handful of fresh flat leaf parsley, finely chopped

500 g/1lb. 2oz. even-sized floury potatoes, such as Maris Piper/Yukon Gold, unpeeled

25 g/3 tablespoons plain/all-purpose flour

70 g/heaping ½ cup rice flour

1½ tablespoons fine polenta

1 egg

100 g/scant ½ cup unsalted butter, melted

OPTIONAL

150 g/2 cups fine dry breadcrumbs

vegetable oil, for frying

TO SERVE

mayonnaise mixed with horseradish

MAKES 20

This is an Austrian recipe that literally translates as 'meat dumplings'. I was a little unsure about how these would turn out, as they don't sound that appetizing but the result was so moreish that they had to be included. I tried them both fried and boiled, and, for me, the slightly less traditional fried ones win hands down. They are a great way to use up leftover roast meat and cured meats such as sausages and salamis.

Heat the oil in a pan and fry the onion until soft and lightly golden. Allow to cool then add to the meat with a good grating of nutmeg and the parsley. Whiz in a food processor to a coarse mixture.

Shape into 20 walnut-sized balls. Cover and chill.

Put the potatoes in their skins in a pan of cold salted water. Bring to the boil and simmer for 20–30 minutes (depending on size) until tender. Drain and, when cool enough to handle, peel off the skins and mash the flesh with a potato ricer (or push it through a large-holed sieve/strainer). Mix it with the rest of the ingredients and season well. Once you have a smooth dough, shape into a log. Wrap in clingfilm/plastic wrap and chill for a couple of hours.

Cut the dough into 20 pieces (about 60 g/2¼ oz.) and shape them around the meatballs.

You can now cook your knödels. Either bring a pan of water to the boil and simmer the knödels for 10 minutes until puffed up, or coat all over with the breadcrumbs, heat a pan of oil 6 cm/2½ in. deep to 170°C (340°F) and fry for 4–5 minutes, turning, until golden brown and crisp all over.

KÄSESPÄTZLE

This is an Austrian version of macaroni cheese that translates as 'little cheese sparrows'. You can buy special spätzle makers – I have a beautiful vintage one that my husband's Austrian granny gave me – but you can use anything with holes, such as a colander or box grater, to make these tasty little morsels. Although this is perfectly delicious as a simple supper, I served these as a side with lemony roast chicken and it made a gorgeous Sunday lunch. You can try adding little pancetta or bacon bits into your onion as you fry for extra flavour. (Pictured on page 18.)

400 g/3 cups plain/all-purpose flour
a good pinch of sea salt
freshly grated nutmeg
5 eggs
125 ml/½ cup water
100 g/scant ½ cup unsalted butter
2 tablespoons vegetable oil
3 large onions, thinly sliced
200 g/1¾ cups grated Alpine melty cheese, such as a mixture of Gruyère and Emmenthal
ground black pepper

SERVES 4 AS A MAIN
OR 6 AS A SIDE

Sift the flour into a bowl with the salt and a good grating of nutmeg. Make a well in the centre and add the eggs. Gradually stir, incorporating the flour, adding the water gradually. You should have a soft dough, almost like a thick batter. Keep beating until bubbles start to appear in the dough. Set aside to rest for about 30 minutes.

Melt 75 g/⅓ cup of the butter and the oil in a large pan and add the onions. Cook over a low heat for 15–20 minutes, stirring regularly until they are an even golden brown. Remove with a slotted spoon and set aside.

Bring a large pan of salted water to the boil. Take dollops of the dough and push through a spätzle maker, colander or the large holes of a grater or potato ricer into the water. You should have little wiggles of pasta in the water. They will all end up different shapes, but don't worry – that is how they should be.

Once they rise to the surface, they are cooked. Scoop out with a slotted spoon into a warm dish and continue cooking the rest of the dough.

Once you have cooked all the spätzle, empty the pan and return the cooked spätzle to it. Toss them with the rest of the butter and the cheese over a low heat until the cheese is melted. Season with plenty of black pepper and tip back into the serving dish. Serve scattered with the golden fried onions.

olive oil, for frying

2 tablespoons plain/all-purpose flour

1.4 kg/3lb. 2oz. wild boar shoulder/butt, cut into large pieces

150 g/5 oz. smoked streaky/fatty bacon, finely chopped

1 large onion, thinly sliced

1 carrot, finely chopped

2 celery sticks, finely chopped

2 bay leaves

10 juniper berries, lightly crushed

a small handful of thyme sprigs

pared zest of 1 lemon

300 ml/generous 1¼ cups red wine

400 g/14 oz. can chopped tomatoes

2 tablespoons tomato purée/paste

300 ml/generous 1¼ cups chicken stock

2 teaspoons red wine vinegar

1 tablespoon crab apple or redcurrant jelly

sea salt and ground black pepper

cooked pappardelle, to serve

SERVES 6

PAPPARDELLE AND BOAR RAGÙ

Wild boar are native to much of Europe but have only recently started to be re-established in the UK. Much of the boar bought in the UK and US is farmed, although there are some wild stocks roaming the countryside, so true wild boar still tends to come from Europe. It has a richer flavour than pork, which works well with the bold flavours of the dish, but if you can't track some down, then use pork shoulder/butt instead. (Pictured opposite.)

Heat a layer of oil in a flameproof casserole over a medium–high heat. Season the flour with plenty of salt and black pepper and dust the wild boar all over. Brown in the casserole in batches, then set aside.

Heat a little more oil in the pan and gently fry the bacon, onion, carrot and celery for 15 minutes until tender and starting to brown. Return the meat to the pan and add the bay, juniper, thyme and lemon zest. Season well then add the red wine, chopped tomatoes, tomato purée/paste, stock and vinegar.

Cover, bring to the boil, then reduce to a simmer and cook for 2–2½ hours until the meat is tender and falls apart when you press it with a spoon. Remove the lid for the last 45 minutes to reduce the sauce to a lovely glossy, thick gravy. Stir in the jelly then serve on al dente pappardelle pasta.

1 tablespoon olive oil, plus extra to drizzle

100 g/3¾ oz. pancetta, finely chopped

1 large onion, finely chopped

1 carrot, finely chopped

1 celery stick, finely chopped

400 g/1¾ cups minced/ground beef

200 g/scant 1 cup minced/ground veal

2 fresh bay leaves

freshly grated nutmeg

200 ml/scant 1 cup red or white wine

3 tablespoons tomato purée/paste

125 ml/½ cup beef stock

100 ml/scant ½ cup whole/full-fat milk

500 g/1lb. 2oz. spaghetti

lots of freshly grated Parmesan, to serve

SERVES 6

SPAGHETTI BOLOGNESE

Bolognese served with spaghetti is a true mountain classic, even though Italians would say this is never allowed because a proper ragù Bolognese should always be served with a flat pasta such as tagliatelle. However, I love the familiar comfort of a spag bol and will risk the wrath of the Italians.

Heat the olive oil in a large pan and fry the pancetta over a high heat until staring to crisp. Add the onion, carrot and celery, and fry over a low heat for about 15–20 minutes until soft and translucent.

Add the minced/ground meat and increase the heat and fry, stirring, until browned all over. Add the bay leaves, a good grating of nutmeg and the wine and bubble for a couple of minutes. Stir in the tomato purée/paste and beef stock, and season well. Partially cover with a lid and simmer on a very low heat for 1½ hours, stirring occasionally and adding a little more stock if it starts to look a bit dry. Add the milk and simmer for a further 20 minutes.

Cook the pasta in boiling salted water for 12–15 minutes until just cooked but still with some bite. Drain and toss with a little olive oil. Serve in warmed bowls and dollop over the ragù. Finish with a good amount of Parmesan.

PIZZOCCHERI

1 savoy cabbage (about 400 g/14 oz.), core removed, thickly shredded

2 large waxy potatoes, sliced into rounds

250 g/9 oz. pizzoccheri or other long buckwheat pasta

1 tablespoon olive oil

50 g/3½ tablespoons unsalted butter, plus extra to garnish

1 banana shallot, thinly sliced

2 garlic cloves, finely chopped

8 sage leaves, plus a few extra to garnish

freshly grated nutmeg

175 g/6 oz. fontina cheese, grated

50 g/¾ cup freshly grated Parmesan

sea salt and ground black pepper

SERVES 6

This was one of the first-ever dishes that I had to shoot when I started work at delicious. magazine – a challenging task, as this is not a pretty dish. But oh my, is it tasty! Traditionally, this recipe uses valtellina casera cheese, but it can be quite hard to find, so I like to use fontina instead.

Bring a large pan of salted water to a rolling boil. Blanch the cabbage for a couple of minutes then remove with a slotted spoon, drain and set aside.

Add the potatoes to the boiling water and cook until they are about to fall apart. Drain and set aside. Add the pasta to the pan and cook for about 12–14 minutes until tender.

Meanwhile, gently heat the oil and butter in a large sauté pan/skillet. Add the shallot, garlic and sage, and fry until soft. Add the cabbage to the pan then, using tongs, remove the pasta from the boiling water and add to the pan. The water clinging to the pasta will emulsify with the butter and coat the pasta. Add a pinch of nutmeg and the fontina and season well. Tip into a serving dish. Heat a grill/broiler to high.

Sprinkle the Parmesan on top and pop under the hot grill/broiler until golden.

Fry a few sage leaves in butter until crisp to garnish the dish, then serve.

BUTTERNUT SQUASH GNOCCHI

1 kg/2¼ lb. butternut squash, peeled and cut into wedges

1 tablespoon olive oil

1 egg

150 g/⅔ cup ricotta cheese

200 g/1⅓ cups 00 flour or potato flour, plus extra to dust

75 g/heaping ½ cup walnuts

75 g/⅓ cup unsalted butter

10 sage leaves

50 g/¾ cup freshly grated Parmesan

sea salt and ground black pepper

SERVES 2–3 AS A MAIN
OR 4 AS A LIGHTER LUNCH

The butternut squash used all over the US and Canada makes a lovely alternative to potato gnocchi. The creamy sweetness of the squash is enhanced by the savouriness of the Parmesan and sage. (Pictured opposite.)

Preheat the oven to 200°C (400°F) Gas 6.

Toss the squash with the oil and season with salt and pepper then roast for 40–45 minutes until tender and slightly caramelized. Mash the squash, then scoop the mash into a colander lined with a clean dishtowel and squeeze out as much water as possible.

Tip into a bowl and mix with the egg and ricotta. Put the flour in a food processor with the walnuts and whiz until the nuts are all ground up. Add to the squash mixture, season and mix until incorporated. Chill in the fridge for 1 hour to make it easier to handle.

On a lightly floured surface, roll into sausage shapes about 1 cm/½ in. thick then cut into 2 cm/¾ in. long pieces. Use the tines on the back of a fork to roll the gnocchi, giving them the characteristic ridges. (You can cook them now or chill for up to 24 hours.)

Bring a large pan of salted water to the boil. Add the gnocchi and cook for 2–3 minutes until they float to the surface. As they cook, melt the butter in a pan and add the sage leaves. Scoop out the gnocchi with a slotted spoon and divide between warmed plates. Spoon over the sage butter, sprinkle with lots of Parmesan and serve.

GNOCCHI WITH WILD MUSHROOMS

500 g/1lb. 2oz. even-sized small floury potatoes, such as Maris Piper/Yukon Gold, unpeeled

100 g/⅔ cup 00 flour, plus extra to dust

freshly grated nutmeg

1 egg, beaten

30 g/2 tablespoons unsalted butter

1 tablespoon olive oil

2 banana shallots, finely chopped

2 garlic cloves, crushed

300 g/11 oz. wild mushrooms, cleaned and sliced if large

75 ml/⅓ cup dry white wine

150 ml/scant ⅔ cup double/heavy cream

a small handful of fresh parsley leaves, chopped

fine sea salt and ground black pepper

freshly grated Parmesan, to serve

SERVES 4–6

There is something undeniably comforting about little pillows of potato gnocchi. When cooked properly, they should be tender and fluffy rather than dense and heavy. If wild mushrooms aren't in season, you can make this with white or portobello mushrooms instead.

Cook the potatoes, whole in their skins, in boiling salted water for 25 minutes until they are tender.

Drain the potatoes and, once cool enough to handle, peel the skins off and mash the flesh using a potato ricer or by pushing it through a sieve/strainer so it is lump-free and fine.

Put the flour, 1 teaspoon salt and a little nutmeg into a bowl and add the potato, mixing with the blade of a knife. Make a well in the centre, add the beaten egg and mix together until well combined. Bring together with your hands but don't knead or you could make your gnocchi tough.

On a lightly floured surface, roll out the dough into sausage shapes, about 1 cm/ ½ in. wide, then cut into 1 cm/ ½ in. pieces. Use the tines on the back of a fork to roll the gnocchi, giving them the characteristic ridges. Put on

a floured baking sheet and chill until you are ready to cook. (You can cook them now or chill for up to 24 hours.)

Make the sauce. Melt the butter in a pan and add the oil and shallots. Cook for 10 minutes until softened and tender. Add the garlic and fry for a further 30 seconds then add the mushrooms. Increase the heat and fry for 10 minutes until they are golden brown.

Add the wine and bubble for a minute. Add the cream, a splash of boiling water to loosen it a little and plenty of salt and pepper, then stir in most of the parsley.

Bring a pan of salted water to the boil and add the gnocchi. They are cooked once they float to the surface, about 1–2 minutes. Scoop out with a slotted spoon and divide among warmed serving bowls. Warm through the sauce and spoon over the gnocchi. Scatter with the remaining parsley and serve.

WARMING SOUPS AND HEARTY STEWS

FRENCH ONION SOUP

25 g/2 tablespoons unsalted butter

3 tablespoons olive oil

1 kg/2¼ lb. large onions, very thinly sliced

250 ml/generous 1 cup dry white wine

1 litre/4⅓ cups rich beef stock

freshly grated nutmeg

a small handful of fresh thyme sprigs

2 fresh bay leaves

75 ml/⅓ cup good-quality Madeira

1 day-old baguette or other crusty bread, cut into slices

1 garlic clove, peeled

150 g/5 oz. Comté cheese, grated

sea salt and ground black pepper

SERVES 4

The key to a perfect French onion soup is to cook your onions for a seriously long time until they are reduced to an unctuous, sticky, golden mass. Rich beef stock and a cheesy croûte top off this classic. (Opposite.)

Melt the butter in a heavy-based pan or flameproof casserole and add the oil. Add the onions and season with salt. Cook over a low heat, stirring occasionally, for at least 45 minutes until they have reduced right down to a golden, sticky mass.

Add the wine and bubble, stirring, for a minute, then add the beef stock, a good grating of nutmeg and the herbs. Simmer for 20 minutes, then add the Madeira and bubble for 5 minutes more.

Check the seasoning and spoon into four small ovenproof bowls or dishes.

Preheat the grill/broiler to high. Toast the slices of crusty bread and rub one side all over with the garlic. Put the toasts on top of the bowls so that they cover the surface of the soup. Sprinkle with lots and lots of cheese and put on a baking sheet under the grill/broiler until the soup is bubbling and the toasts are oozingly melted and golden. Serve straight away.

BEER SOUP

300 g/11 oz. rye bread, cubed

660 ml/2¾ cups beer (lager or golden beer)

600 ml/2½ cups beef stock

a good glug of double/heavy cream, to taste

a handful of fresh chives, finely chopped

75 g/3 oz. raclette cheese, cut into little cubes

SERVES 6

An unusual idea perhaps, but this speciality of the Valais region of the Swiss Alps really hits the spot when it's cold outside. The hoppy flavour of the beer mingles with the deep richness of the rye bread. You can use any type of mountain cheese, such as Comté or Gruyère, but raclette cheese adds its own unique flavour to the soup.

Soak the cubed rye bread in the beer for half an hour, then whiz it all up to a smooth mixture in a food processor or blender.

Heat the beef stock then add the bread and beer. Simmer for 15–20 minutes. Stir in the cream and chives. Serve in warm bowls, scattered with pieces of cheese.

SOUPE AUX CAILLOUX

50 g/3½ tablespoons unsalted butter

200 g/7 oz. smoked bacon lardons

1 green cabbage, thinly sliced

2 potatoes (about 350 g/12 oz.), chopped

1 leek, sliced on the diagonal

3 carrots, finely chopped

2 small turnips, finely chopped

3 celery sticks, finely chopped

1.75 litres/7¾ cups vegetable stock
or water

2 large clean stones or pebbles,
not too rounded

SERVES 6

Stone soup – a rich vegetable soup, sometimes with smoked sausage or bacon – traditionally used a large, clean stone to help to break down the vegetables in the days before blenders. Of course, you don't actually have to use a couple of stones, as in this recipe; if you prefer, you can just use a potato masher to smash up some of the vegetables at the end of cooking, but it's far more fun to do it the traditional way!

Melt the butter in a flameproof casserole and add the bacon. Fry until starting to become golden.

Add the vegetables and cook, stirring, until softened. Pour in the stock and season well.

Drop in the stones and bring to a vigorous simmer. Simmer for 2 hours with the lid on, until the stones have broken down the vegetables and you have a rich, thick soup. Serve with crusty baguette and Beaufort cheese.

POTÉE

1 unsmoked ham hock, about 1.2 kg/2¾ lb.

1 onion, halved

2 bay leaves

a handful of fresh thyme sprigs

10 black peppercorns

2 small leeks, sliced into bite-sized pieces

2 carrots, sliced into bite-sized pieces

2 celery sticks, finely chopped

300 g/11 oz. potatoes, cut into bite-sized pieces

1 small turnip, cut into bite-sized pieces

2 tablespoons olive oil

160 g/5½ oz. smoked bacon lardons

6 Toulouse or other herby sausages

1 small savoy cabbage, shredded

extra virgin olive oil and freshly chopped chives, to serve (optional)

SERVES 4

Referring to the earthenware pot it is traditionally cooked in, potée is a stew of meat and vegetables. It is real peasant fare, made using whatever is to hand, and often this is pork shoulder or ham hock with smoked sausage and vegetables, such as turnip, potatoes and cabbage. It's a pork and cabbage hotpot, if you will. (Pictured opposite.)

Put the ham hock in a pan with the onion, bay, thyme and peppercorns. Cover with 2–2½ litres/8¾–10½ cups cold water and bring to a simmer. Cook for 1½ hours until really tender.

Remove the hock and strain the stock into a clean pan. Bring the stock back to the boil and add the vegetables. Simmer for 15 minutes until just tender.

Meanwhile, heat the oil in a frying pan/skillet and fry the lardons until golden. Set aside.

Add the sausages to the pan and fry until golden brown all over. Slice the sausages into pieces.

Shred the meat from the ham hock and add this, the bacon and sausages to the pan with the vegetables. Add the savoy cabbage and cook for a further 5 minutes.

To serve, spoon into large bowls, drizzle with extra virgin olive oil and scatter with freshly chopped chives, if you like.

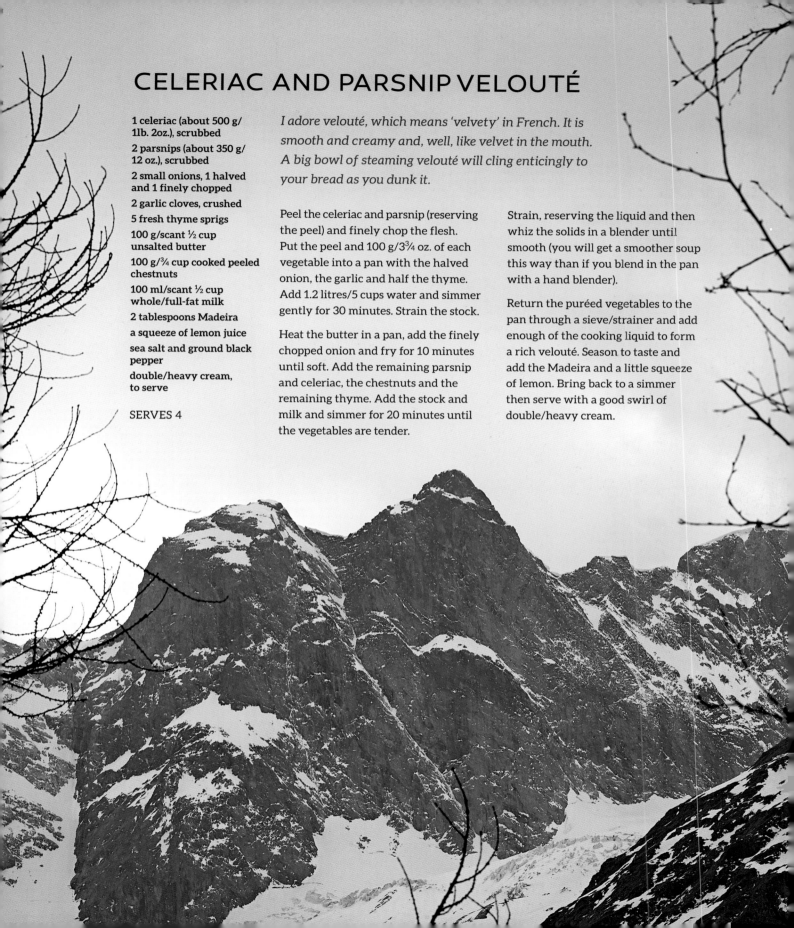

CELERIAC AND PARSNIP VELOUTÉ

1 celeriac (about 500 g/
1lb. 2oz.), scrubbed

2 parsnips (about 350 g/
12 oz.), scrubbed

2 small onions, 1 halved
and 1 finely chopped

2 garlic cloves, crushed

5 fresh thyme sprigs

100 g/scant ½ cup
unsalted butter

100 g/¾ cup cooked peeled
chestnuts

100 ml/scant ½ cup
whole/full-fat milk

2 tablespoons Madeira

a squeeze of lemon juice

sea salt and ground black
pepper

double/heavy cream,
to serve

SERVES 4

I adore velouté, which means 'velvety' in French. It is smooth and creamy and, well, like velvet in the mouth. A big bowl of steaming velouté will cling enticingly to your bread as you dunk it.

Peel the celeriac and parsnip (reserving the peel) and finely chop the flesh. Put the peel and 100 g/3¾ oz. of each vegetable into a pan with the halved onion, the garlic and half the thyme. Add 1.2 litres/5 cups water and simmer gently for 30 minutes. Strain the stock.

Heat the butter in a pan, add the finely chopped onion and fry for 10 minutes until soft. Add the remaining parsnip and celeriac, the chestnuts and the remaining thyme. Add the stock and milk and simmer for 20 minutes until the vegetables are tender.

Strain, reserving the liquid and then whiz the solids in a blender until smooth (you will get a smoother soup this way than if you blend in the pan with a hand blender).

Return the puréed vegetables to the pan through a sieve/strainer and add enough of the cooking liquid to form a rich velouté. Season to taste and add the Madeira and a little squeeze of lemon. Bring back to a simmer then serve with a good swirl of double/heavy cream.

GOULASH SOUP

olive oil, to fry

100 g/3¾ oz. smoked streaky/fatty bacon, finely chopped

1 kg/2¼ lb. braising steak or beef shin, cut into 2.5 cm/1 in. chunks

2 heaped tablespoons plain/all-purpose flour

2 large onions, thinly sliced

2 red peppers/bell peppers, deseeded and sliced

3 garlic cloves, crushed

5 juniper berries, crushed

2 bay leaves

1 tablespoon sweet smoked paprika

½ tablespoon hot paprika

2 teaspoons caraway seeds

2 tablespoons tomato purée/paste

1 tablespoon red wine vinegar

1.2 litres/5 cups beef stock

300 g/11 oz. waxy potatoes, cut into chunks

2 beetroot/beets, cut into chunks

sea salt and ground black pepper

freshly chopped parsley and sour cream, to serve

SERVES 6

This Hungarian dish spread into the mountains, where it is always popular in the huts and cabins as a hearty meal on the slopes and trails. There is a healthy kick of paprika with the added richness of sour cream, which helps to make this one of the most warming and comforting dishes. This is also delicious made with pork instead of beef – use a slow-cook cut such as shoulder/butt and cut it into large chunks.

Heat a good layer of olive oil in a flameproof casserole or large saucepan and fry the bacon over a medium heat until starting to colour. Remove with a slotted spoon and set aside.

Dust the beef in the flour with plenty of seasoning, then brown in batches over a high heat in the same pan, adding more oil if necessary. Remove and set aside with the bacon.

Add a little more oil to the pan and add the onions and peppers/bell peppers. Fry for 10 minutes until softened and the onions start to colour. Add the garlic, juniper, bay and spices, and fry for a few minutes before adding the tomato purée/paste, vinegar and stock.

Return the beef and bacon to the pan and season well. Bring to a simmer, then cover and cook for 2–2½ hours until the beef is starting to become really tender.

Add the potatoes and beetroot/beets to the pan and simmer, with the lid off, until the vegetables are tender.

Stir in the parsley and serve in large warmed bowls with generous dollops of sour cream.

DIOT COOKED IN WHITE WINE WITH CROZETS

1 tablespoon olive oil

8 diot or other cured pork sausages

a knob/pat of unsalted butter

2 onions, thinly sliced

2 teaspoons plain/all-purpose flour

350 ml/1½ cups white wine

2 bay leaves

200 g/1¾ cups crozet or small pasta

150 ml/scant ⅔ cup double/heavy cream

50 g/2 oz. Comté cheese, grated

a handful of dried breadcrumbs

sea salt and ground black pepper

SERVES 4

A diot is a pork, or often pork and cabbage, sausage from the Savoie region of the French Alps. The sausages are cured and can be eaten raw, but more often they are cooked in white wine. Crozets are small squares of pasta made with buckwheat. Both ingredients are a little tricky to track down but are well worth it if you can. Online is the best place. (Opposite.)

Heat the olive oil in a pan and brown the diot all over. Set aside. Add the butter to the pan and then the onions. Fry over a low heat until they are soft and golden, about 20 minutes.

Add the flour and cook for 1 minute, then add the wine and bay leaves, and return the sausages to the pan. Cover and cook for 15–20 minutes, turning once.

Meanwhile, preheat the grill/broiler to high. Cook the pasta in boiling salted water for 15 minutes, then drain. Mix the pasta with the cream, cheese and plenty of seasoning, and tip into an ovenproof dish.

Scatter with the crumbs and pop under the grill/broiler until golden brown. Serve with the diot in white wine.

ROCKY MOUNTAIN STEW

1 kg/2¼ lb. skirt steak (bavette) or other braising steak, cut into pieces

4 tablespoons plain/all-purpose flour, seasoned

vegetable oil, to fry

500 ml/2 cups beef stock

1 teaspoon paprika

1 garlic clove, crushed

a pinch of sugar

2 tablespoons Worcestershire sauce

1 bay leaf

400 g/14 oz. potatoes, diced

1 large carrot, diced

300 g/11 oz. baby onions or very small shallots, peeled

sea salt and ground black pepper

SERVES 4–6

You may have heard of rocky mountain oysters, which bear absolutely no resemblance to any kind of sea-dwelling mollusc but are in fact bull's testicles. These are often turned into a hearty braise or stew, but apart from being a little hard to source they are not for the faint-hearted! This stew takes its flavours from a traditional rocky mountain oyster stew but uses beef steak instead. (Pictured on page 41.)

Dust the beef all over with the seasoned flour. Heat a layer of oil in a large flameproof casserole and brown the beef all over in batches.

Return all the beef to the pan and pour over the stock. Add the paprika, garlic, sugar, Worcestershire sauce and bay leaf. Cover and leave to simmer very gently for 2 hours.

Add the potatoes, carrot, baby onions and a good splash of water, and simmer, partially covered with the lid, for a further 20 minutes until the vegetables are tender and the meat falls apart if you push it with a spoon.

Serve with creamy mashed potatoes or baked/jacket potatoes.

ZÜRCHER GESCHNETZELTES

2 tablespoons olive oil

500 g/1lb. 2oz. veal escalope, beef sirloin or pork tenderloin, cut into thin strips

2 tablespoons plain/all-purpose flour, seasoned

20 g/1½ tablespoons unsalted butter

1 small onion, finely chopped

200 g/3⅓ cups button/white mushrooms, sliced

2 garlic cloves, sliced

125ml/½ cup white wine

finely grated zest of 1 lemon, and a squeeze of the juice

100 ml/scant ½ cup double/heavy cream

1 teaspoon paprika

freshly chopped parsley, to garnish

sea salt and ground black pepper

SERVES 4

An elegant and rich Swiss dish from Zurich, this dish is similar to stroganoff. There are lots of versions of this dish, but I wanted to keep it simple. Veal is traditionally used, but you can use beef or pork just as easily. (Opposite.)

Heat the oil in a large nonstick frying pan/skillet. Dust the meat in the seasoned flour, then fry in batches, until browned all over, adding a splash more oil if you need to. Remove with a slotted spoon and set aside. Deglaze the pan with a splash of water and reserve the liquid.

Add the butter to the pan and fry the onion for 5 minutes over a medium heat. Add the mushrooms, increase the heat, season and cook until the mushrooms are golden. Add the garlic and cook for 30 seconds.

Return the meat and juices to the pan and pour in the wine, bubble for a minute then add the lemon zest, cream, reserved deglazing water to loosen and the paprika. Simmer for 3 minutes then serve scattered with lots of parsley and a squeeze of lemon juice and with creamy mash, rice or noodles.

CARBONADE

olive oil, for frying

1.2–1.4.kg/2½–3lb. 2oz. piece uncooked salt beef, cut into large pieces

2 tablespoons plain/all-purpose flour seasoned

50 g/3½ tablespoons unsalted butter

3 large onions, sliced

500 ml/2 cups full-bodied Italian red wine

500 ml/2 cups beef stock

3 cloves

2 bay leaves

1 cinnamon stick

4 fresh thyme sprigs

freshly grated nutmeg

sea salt and ground black pepper

SERVES 6

Traditional in the Aosta Valley that borders the Rhone Alps, this is a dish of salt beef cooked with onions, herbs, spices and lots of red wine, served with polenta or bread. The French version of this dish – carbonnade (with a double 'n') – is usually cooked in beer or ale. If you can't find the uncooked salt beef, you can just use braising steak instead. (Pictured on page 44.)

Heat a little oil in a large non-stick frying pan/skillet. Dust the meat in the seasoned flour, then fry in batches, until browned all over, adding a splash more oil if you need to. Remove with a slotted spoon and set aside.

Heat a little more oil in the pan and add the butter, onions and a good pinch of salt. Cook over a low heat for 15 minutes until softened and lightly golden.

Return the beef pieces to the pan and add the red wine, stock, cloves, bay leaves, cinnamon, thyme and a good grating of nutmeg, and season with salt and pepper.

Bring to a simmer, then cover and cook for about 3 hours until the meat is tender and falling apart.

Serve with creamy polenta (page 63).

CASSOULET

Although it hails from the south of France, this slow-cooked dish of beans, pork and confit duck is more at home in colder climes to warm the cockles and energize weary skiers and trekkers. The breadcrumbs on the top absorb the fat, making a delicious, golden crust that hides a soft underbelly of tender meat and garlic-infused beans.

750 g/4¼ cups dried haricot/navy beans, soaked overnight in cold water

150 g/5 oz. pancetta cubes

1 onion, halved

4 garlic cloves, lightly crushed

2 bay leaves

5 fresh thyme sprigs

2 confit duck legs in fat (see page 104)

6 Toulouse sausages

750 g/1 lb. 10 oz. boneless pork belly, cut into cubes

2–3 tablespoons tomato purée/paste, to taste

150 g/3 cups fresh breadcrumbs

sea salt and ground black pepper

SERVES 8

Drain the beans and tip them into a large flameproof casserole. Cover with cold water so that it comes up to about 4 cm/1½ in. above the level of the beans. Mix in the pancetta, onion, garlic, bay and thyme. Cover with a lid and simmer gently for 1 hour or so until the beans are starting to become tender.

Meanwhile, remove the duck legs from the fat, reserving the fat. Heat a tablespoon or so of the duck fat in a large frying pan/skillet and brown the duck legs, sausages and pork belly, adding more duck fat if necessary. Cut the sausages into pieces and shred the duck legs and discard the bones.

Preheat the oven to 150°C (300°F) Gas 2.

Once the beans are just cooked, remove and discard the onion and herbs. Season with salt and pepper. Stir in the tomato purée/paste and all the browned meat. Sprinkle with a layer of the breadcrumbs and cook in the oven for 2–2½ hours. Check on it every so often. Once a crust has formed, stir it into the cassoulet then sprinkle with some more breadcrumbs and keep cooking. You should have a lovely thick golden crust at the end of cooking.

Leave to stand for 10–15 minutes before serving.

OOZING CHEESE AND CREAMY BAKES

CROÛTE AU FROMAGE

2 thick-cut slices of slightly stale white bread

2 tablespoons softened unsalted butter

4 tablespoons dry white wine

2 slices air-dried ham

200 g/7 oz. raclette cheese, especially the rindy bits, or any cheese you have in the fridge

gherkins and pickled silverskin onions, to serve

SERVES 2

Here is a Swiss take on cheese on toast – and what a take it is. Not an everyday cheese toastie, but a special-occasion, treat-yourself cheese toastie. Thick-cut bread is toasted in butter in a pan, then sprinkled with white wine and covered in cheese (usually the rindy ends of raclette or other melting cheese) and baked. Heaven. (Pictured opposite.)

Heat the grill/broiler to high and heat a frying pan/skillet over a medium heat.

Butter the bread on both sides, then fry until golden. Put each one in a little gratin dish and sprinkle with the white wine. Top with the slices of ham and the cheese. Pop the dishes under the grill/broiler until golden and bubbling.

Serve the croûte with plenty of pickles on the side.

MAC 'N' CHEESE

500 g/scant 4¼ cups macaroni

50 g/3½ tablespoons unsalted butter

40 g/4¾ tablespoons plain/all-purpose flour

600 ml/generous 2½ cups whole/full-fat milk

freshly grated nutmeg

1 teaspoon English mustard powder

100 g/heaping 1 cup grated Cheddar cheese

100 g/1 cup grated firm mozzarella cheese

2 tablespoons freshly grated Parmesan

3 tablespoons fresh breadcrumbs

sea salt and ground black pepper

SERVES 6

Simple and classic this dish needs very little explanation. An all-time American classic, comfort food at its very best. No frills, no fuss, just cheese.

Preheat the oven to 180°C (350°F) Gas 4.

Cook the pasta in a large pan of boiling salted water for 8–10 minutes until almost cooked but still al dente.

Meanwhile, melt the butter in a pan, add the flour and cook for 2 minutes. Gradually stir in the milk, making a thick white sauce. Season and add a good grating of nutmeg, the mustard, Cheddar and mozzarella.

Scoop the pasta out of the pan with a slotted spoon and add to the cheese sauce. Mix well.

Tip into a large ovenproof dish. Mix together the grated Parmesan and the breadcrumbs, and sprinkle over the top of the dish.

Bake in the preheated oven for about 15–20 minutes until golden and bubbling, then serve.

TRADITIONAL CHEESE FONDUE

1 fat garlic clove, halved

2 teaspoons cornflour/cornstarch

400 ml/1¾ cups hoppy lager beer

800 g/7 cups grated mixture of Swiss or French Alpine cheeses, such as Gruyère or Comté, Vacherin Fribourgeois, good-quality Emmenthal and Beaufort – choose two or three cheeses

1–2 teaspoons whisky, to taste

1 large loaf of slightly stale country white bread, cut into cubes

gherkins, pickled silverskin onions and charcuterie, to serve

SERVES 6–8

Made with a melange of cheeses, a true Swiss fondue is a mixture of Gruyère and Vacherin Fribourgeois – a semi-hard cheese with a lovely nutty flavour. Traditionally, it is melted with white wine and grappa or kirsch and served with chunks of bread to dip into it alongside charcuterie and pickles. I like to make a more subtle version with beer and whisky, making it even more delicious, if that is possible. You really do need a fondue pot for the best results, as the pot sits above a flame that keeps the cheese melted and gently bubbling. They are really easy to pick up quite cheaply second-hand. (Pictured opposite.)

Rub the garlic all over the inside of a fondue pot. Mix the cornflour/cornstarch with a little of the beer to make a smooth paste, then add this and the rest of the beer to the pot.

Put over a low heat, add the cheese and stir until it is melted and steaming but not boiling. If it is too thick you can add a little more beer. Add the whisky and then transfer to the fondue stand and light the burner.

Dip the slightly stale bread into the melting cheese and eat with lots of pickles and charcuterie.

POUTINE

1 kg/2¼ lb. red-skinned potatoes, cut into fries

vegetable oil, to deep-fry

2 tablespoons cornflour/cornstarch

2 tablespoons water

100 g/scant ½ cup unsalted butter

1 garlic clove, crushed

400 ml/1¾ cups rich beef stock

200 ml/scant 1 cup brown chicken stock

1 tablespoon Worcestershire sauce

300 g/11 oz. curd cheese or firm mozzarella, torn into chunks

SERVES 6

A peculiarly Canadian dish, poutine is held dear to their hearts. Think cheesy chips but better – a twice-cooked chip smothered in a rich gravy and tangy curd cheese. We haven't quite caught up with the curd-cheese passion over in the UK, although it is now becoming available in major supermarkets, but don't be disheartened, if you can't find curd cheese, try using a firm mozzarella torn into pieces.

Put the potatoes in a bowl of cold water and chill for a couple of hours.

Drain the potatoes and pat dry. Heat a deep-fryer or pan of oil about 7.5 cm/ 3 in. deep to 150°C (300°F). Cook the fries for 3–4 minutes until lightly golden. Remove and drain on paper towels.

Mix the cornflour/cornstarch with the water. Melt the butter in a pan, add the garlic and cook for 30 seconds. Stir in the cornflour/cornstarch mixture and cook for 1–2 minutes. Gradually stir in the stocks and Worcestershire sauce. Simmer until glossy and thick. Keep hot.

Increase the temperature of the oil in the pan to 190°C (375°F) and fry the part-cooked fries for 4–5 minutes more until golden and brown. Drain and tip into a serving bowl.

Dot the fries all over with the curds or mozzarella and pour over the hot gravy, then serve immediately.

TARTIFLETTE

1 kg/2¼ lb. large waxy potatoes, unpeeled

a knob/pat of unsalted butter

200 g/7 oz. smoked bacon lardons

1 garlic clove, thinly sliced

75 ml/scant ⅓ cup dry white wine

200 ml/scant 1 cup double/heavy cream

300 g/11 oz. Reblochon cheese, thickly sliced

sea salt and ground black pepper

SERVES 6

One of the most iconic mountain recipes, tartiflette is beloved by skiers and non-skiers alike. Melting Reblochon cheese smothering firm, waxy potatoes makes this a bubbling dish of heaven. Traditionalists would insist that the dish contains just cheese, potatoes and bacon, but I like to add a good glug of cream, which loosens the dish and gives it extra-creamy depth. (Opposite.)

Preheat the oven to 190°C (375°F) Gas 5.

Cook the potatoes in a pan of boiling salted water for 10–12 minutes, until just tender. Drain, thickly slice and set aside.

Heat the butter in a frying pan/skillet and fry the lardons until starting to crisp. Add the garlic and wine and bubble until the wine is almost gone.

Season, remove from the heat and stir through the cream and potato slices.

Layer the potato mixture with most of the cheese slices in a large ovenproof dish, pouring over any remaining cream from the pan at the end, before topping with a final layer of cheese.

Bake in the oven for 25–30 minutes until golden and bubbling.

GRATIN DAUPHINOISE

1 garlic clove, halved

softened butter, for greasing

1 kg/2¼ lb. floury potatoes such as Maris Piper/Yukon Gold, very thinly sliced

600 ml/generous 2½ cups double/heavy cream

freshly grated nutmeg

sea salt and ground black pepper

SERVES 6

This is, perhaps, the most famous potato dish there is: tender cream-laced potatoes. It's the ultimate side dish. I like to use floury potatoes, because they give a lovely soft texture, but others prefer waxy potatoes for a more toothsome finish. This is the dish in its simplest form, and I think it is perfect as it is, but you can always add an embellishment or two, such as a grating of Gruyère cheese, some softened onion or crispy pieces of bacon.

Preheat the oven to 160°C (325°F) Gas 3.

Rub the inside of a large ovenproof dish with the garlic, then grease with the softened butter.

Layer the potatoes in the prepared ovenproof dish, with lots of salt and pepper in between the layers.

Put the cream in a pan and bring just up to the boil, then remove from the heat and add a good grating of nutmeg.

Pour the cream mixture over the potatoes, then bake in the oven for 1½ hours until the potatoes are tender and the top is golden and bubbling.

FARCEMENT

50 g/3½ tablespoons unsalted butter, melted, plus extra to grease

26 slices smoked streaky/fatty bacon

150 g/5 oz. bacon lardons

1 large onion, thinly sliced

10 ready-to-eat pitted prunes, halved

75 g/½ cup sultanas/golden raisins

1 kg/2¼ lb. floury potatoes, such as Maris Piper/Yukon Gold

freshly grated nutmeg

salt and ground black pepper

20-cm/8-in. round ovenproof dish or cake pan

SERVES 8–10

I first ate farcement in a little piste-side restaurant in Les Houches in Chamonix as the snow bucketed down outside. Instantly, I fell in love with this traditional Savoie dish, and for once there is not a grating of cheese in sight. You can buy farcement moulds, but an ovenproof dish works just as well. It is lined with bacon and filled with potato, fried onions and lardons, prunes and raisins, then slow-cooked to perfection. (Pictured on page 59.)

Preheat the oven to 180°C (350°F) Gas 4.

Take half the butter and rub it around the inside of the ovenproof dish or cake pan. Stretch the slices of bacon out a little with the back of a knife. Line the base of the dish, overlapping them slightly, with two-thirds of the rashers of bacon so that they come up the sides and overhang the edge of the dish.

Fry the lardons in a dry pan until golden, then tip into a bowl with the fat. Add the sliced onion, prunes and sultanas/golden raisins.

Coarsely grate the potatoes. Place in a clean dishtowel and squeeze out as much liquid as possible, then add to the bowl. Add the remaining melted butter, a good grating of nutmeg and seasoning, then spoon into the dish and press down.

Bring the overhanging bacon over the top of the filling to enclose it, using the remaining slices to cover the top. Cover with a buttered piece of foil, put in a roasting pan and pour boiling water around the outside until it comes half way up the sides. Bake for 2½–3 hours. Serve hot, sliced into thick pieces.

SWISS CHARD GRATIN

800 g/1¾ lb. Swiss chard

50 g/3½ tablespoons butter

75 g/½ cup plus 1 tablespoon plain/all-purpose flour

200 ml/scant 1 cup crème fraîche

300 ml/1¼ cups double/heavy cream

freshly grated nutmeg

50 g/1 cup fresh breadcrumbs

finely grated zest of 1 lemon and a good squeeze of juice

50 g/heaping ½ cup grated Gruyère cheese

1 tablespoon olive oil

sea salt and ground black pepper

SERVES 6

My gratin is iron-rich and full of goodness, only somewhat negated by the cream and cheese! This gratin is great as a meal in itself with a little added bacon if you want a meaty hit. (Pictured opposite.)

Preheat the grill/broiler to medium. Bring a pan of water to the boil and blanch the chard for 2–3 minutes, then drain and refresh under cold running water. Squeeze out as much of the water as possible and set aside.

Melt the butter in a pan, add the flour and cook for 1–2 minutes. Add the crème fraîche, cream and a good grating of nutmeg. Simmer for 2–3 minutes. Season.

Mix the breadcrumbs with the lemon zest, cheese and olive oil.

Mix the chard and the sauce together. Spoon the chard into a large ovenproof dish. Sprinkle with the breadcrumbs, then put under the grill/broiler for a couple of minutes until golden brown and bubbling. (If you like, you can mix the sauce with the chard and leave until ready to cook. Heat through in a medium oven for 5–10 minutes before browning under the grill/broiler.)

Serve with a squeeze of lemon juice.

SOFT POLENTA

1.5 litres/6½ cups chicken or vegetable stock

300 g/2 cups quick-cook polenta

150 g/5 oz. Beaufort or Gruyère cheese, grated

75 g/⅓ cup unsalted butter

SERVES 6

A pot of lava-like polenta seems to sing as it merrily bubbles away. These days, fast-cook polenta greatly speeds up the process so that you can have a cheese-laced dish ready in minutes. Scoop any leftovers into a flat dish and allow it to cool, then you can slice it up and fry the pieces to make golden and crisp little fingers. (Pictured opposite.)

Bring the stock to the boil and quickly tip in the polenta. Bubble, stirring, for 3–4 minutes until thick and smooth.

Beat in the cheese and butter and season with lots of black pepper and a little salt if it needs it.

RACLETTE

1.2 kg/2½ lb. waxy new potatoes

1 kg/2¼ lb. piece raclette cheese

gherkins, pickled silverskin onions, cured meats and salamis, to serve

sea salt and ground black pepper

FOR THE TOMATO SALAD

6 large vine tomatoes, sliced

1 garlic clove, crushed

1 tablespoon red wine vinegar

a good pinch of sugar

4 tablespoons extra virgin olive oil

2 tablespoons freshly chopped parsley leaves

FOR THE GREEN SALAD

2 tablespoons white wine or cider vinegar

1 teaspoon Dijon mustard

4 tablespoons extra virgin olive oil

2 tablespoons crème fraîche

1 large head of soft green lettuce

raclette grill

SERVES 6

The word raclette is the name of an incredible Swiss cheese and the dish you use it for. Raclette cheese is a washed-rind, extremely melty cheese that comes in large wheels. All over Switzerland, villages have their own style of raclette cheese, and each village hotly contests that theirs is the best. A layer from a wedge of the cheese is melted against a heated element and scraped off using a spatula (the word racleur meaning to 'scrape') onto awaiting just-boiled potatoes. It is served with air-dried hams and salamis, cornichons and pickled silverskin onions. Make sure you eat the rindy bits and don't push them to one side, as they are packed with the best flavour.

Cook the potatoes in boiling salted water until tender. Drain well. Line a bowl with a clean dishtowel, tip the potatoes into it and wrap them up to keep warm.

Meanwhile, make the salads. Put the tomatoes on a platter. Whisk the garlic, red wine vinegar, sugar and seasoning in a small bowl then gradually add the oil. Pour over the tomatoes and scatter with the parsley.

Whisk the vinegar and mustard together with plenty of seasoning. Whisk in the oil and crème fraîche. Loosen with a little water if you need to.

Wash the lettuce and put in a serving bowl. Pour over the dressing and toss.

Melt the exposed side of the raclette cheese against the grill of a raclette machine. Once melting and bubbling, put a few potatoes on a plate and scrape a layer of the cheesy goodness on top of the potatoes. Repeat for the next plate.

Eat with the salads, the cured meats and pickles.

HEAVEN AND EARTH PIE

4 large waxy potatoes (about 750 g/
1 lb. 10 oz.)

a good knob/pat of unsalted butter

2 tablespoons vegetable oil or olive oil

2 onions, finely chopped

1 leek, thinly sliced

2 Cox's or russet apples, peeled, cored
and sliced

1 firm but ripe pear

200 g/7 oz. raclette cheese or other cheese,
such as Beaufort, coarsely grated

plain/all-purpose flour, to dust

2 × 375 g/13 oz. packs all-butter puff pastry

1 egg, beaten

sea salt and ground black pepper

SERVES 6

I have changed the name of this dish, which is more traditionally called cholera pie. It is thought to have originated from the 1830s when cholera swept through Switzerland and people couldn't leave their homes, so they packed whatever food they had into a pastry crust. Here, potatoes from the ground represent the earth, and apples from the trees that reach to the sky represent the heaven.

Cook the potatoes in boiling salted water until tender then drain and leave to cool completely. You can do this the day before and chill in the fridge. Slice into thin rounds.

Heat the butter and oil in a pan and gently fry the onions and leek for 20 minutes until lovely and tender and slightly golden. Remove from the pan with a slotted spoon and set aside. Add the apples and pear to the pan, with another knob of butter, and cook over a medium-high heat until lightly golden and softened. Mix with the onion and cool completely.

On a lightly floured surface, roll out one of the sheets of pastry and cut a 24 cm/9½ in. diameter circle. Put on a baking sheet. Put a layer of one-third of the potatoes in the centre of the pastry, leaving a 2 cm/¾ in. border. Top with half the onion mix then scatter with half the cheese. Repeat this layering, then top with a final layer of potato.

Roll out the other sheet of pastry into a 28 cm/11 in. circle. Brush the exposed rim of the bottom pastry with egg and then lay over the larger sheet. Use your fingers to press the edges together, then trim to neaten. Crimp with your fingers and brush all over with beaten egg. Use the back of a sharp knife to mark the top of the pastry, then chill for 20 minutes.

Preheat the oven to 200°C (400°F) Gas 6. Bake the pie for 30–35 minutes until golden and crisp. Leave to cool for 10 minutes then serve.

ZWIEBELKUCHEN

10 g/¼ oz. fresh yeast (or ½ × 7 g/¼ oz. sachet dried yeast)

125 ml/½ cup semi-skimmed/low-fat milk, just-warm

175 g/1⅓ cups plain/all-purpose flour

½ teaspoon fine sea salt

25 g/2 tablespoons unsalted butter, melted and cooled

1 egg yolk

FOR THE FILLING

25 g/2 tablespoons unsalted butter

500 g/1lb. 2oz. onions, thinly sliced

½ teaspoon caraway seeds

150 ml/scant ⅔ cup sour cream

1 egg

sea salt

35 x 25-cm/14 x 10-in. roasting pan, lined with baking parchment

SERVES 4 FOR LUNCH
WITH A SALAD

This delightful onion bread (as it literally means) is something of a cross between a tart and a pizza, the soft, squidgy dough melds with the tender sweet onions and the tang of sour cream. (Pictured opposite.)

Mix the yeast with 45 ml/3 tablespoons of the warm milk and leave until it is frothy. Tip the flour into a bowl with the salt. Make a well in the centre and add the yeast, the remaining milk, melted butter and egg yolk. Mix until you have a soft, slightly sticky dough. Knead well on a lightly floured surface for 10 minutes then put in a clean bowl and cover with lightly greased clingfilm/plastic wrap and leave in a warm place for 1 hour or until doubled in size.

Meanwhile, melt the butter for the filling in a pan and fry the onions with the caraway seeds and a good pinch of salt over a low heat for 35–40 minutes

until really softened and golden brown. Tip into a bowl to cool.

Preheat the oven to 200°C (400°F) Gas 6.

Roll out the dough and use to line the prepared roasting pan. Leave to prove, covered in lightly greased clingfilm/plastic wrap for 15–20 minutes.

Mix the onions with the sour cream and eggs. Spread over the top of the dough and leave to prove for 10–15 minutes.

Bake in the preheated oven for about 30–35 minutes until golden. Cool on a wire rack. Serve slightly warm or at room temperature.

SPINACH AND ANCHOVY TART

175 g/1⅓ cups plain/all-purpose flour, plus extra to dust

85 g/⅓ cup plus 2 teaspoons unsalted butter, diced

a good pinch of sea salt

1–2 tablespoons cold water

FOR THE FILLING

600 g/1 lb. 5 oz. spinach

30 g/2 tablespoons unsalted butter, melted

freshly grated nutmeg

2 eggs

150 g/⅔ cup soft cheese/cream cheese

40 g/scant ⅓ cup grated Gruyère cheese

100 ml/scant ½ cup double/heavy cream

6 anchovy fillets, finely chopped

sea salt and ground black pepper

20-cm/8-in. fluted tart pan

SERVES 4–6

Sometimes, the simplest dishes are the most delicious. I made this for a good friend who claims not to be fond of anchovies, but she was won over by this tempting tart. The anchovy flavour is a subtle salty background hint.

Put the flour, diced butter and salt in a bowl and rub in with your fingertips until they resemble breadcrumbs. Add the water and bring together, then knead briefly into a dough. Shape into a disc and chill for 15 minutes.

On a lightly floured surface, roll out the pastry and line the tart pan. Chill for 10–15 minutes. Preheat the oven to 200°C (400°F) Gas 6.

Line the tart case with baking parchment and baking beans or rice and blind bake for 12–15 minutes. Remove the paper

and beans and bake for 5 minutes more until lightly golden. Set aside to cool.

Place the spinach in a colander in the sink and pour over boiling water to wilt. Refresh under cold water, then squeeze out as much liquid as possible. Roughly chop, then put in a bowl and add the melted butter, a good grating of nutmeg, a little salt, lots of pepper and the rest of the ingredients. Mix well. Reduce the oven temperature to 180°C (350°F) Gas 4.

Pour the filling into the case. Bake for 25–30 minutes until just set. Serve warm.

LUNCH, BRUNCH AND SMALL PLATES

SALAD PAYSANNE

'Peasant salad' seems to me like a misnomer, as it is filled with all kinds of delicious goodies – those mountain peasants of old really do seem to have had all the best ingredients lying around!

500 g/1lb. 2oz. new potatoes

200 g/7 oz. smoked bacon lardons

1 tablespoon olive oil

a knob of butter

75 g/3 oz. stale crusty bread, torn into pieces

4 eggs

75 g/3 oz. Comté cheese, cut into small cubes

4 vine cherry tomatoes, sliced

a small bunch of fresh chives, chopped

½ frisée lettuce, torn

FOR THE DRESSING

2 teaspoons Dijon mustard

1 garlic clove, crushed

a pinch of sugar

2 tablespoons red wine vinegar

4 tablespoons extra virgin olive oil

sea salt and ground black pepper

SERVES 4

Cook the potatoes in boiling, salted water for 15–20 minutes until tender. Drain and slice. Put in a serving bowl.

Heat a frying pan/skillet over a medium heat and fry the lardons until they are golden and crisp and have released all their fat. Scoop from the pan and add to the potatoes, leaving the fat in the pan.

Add the olive oil and butter to the pan with the bacon fat and add the torn bread. Fry until golden and crisp. Toss with the potatoes.

Make the dressing by whisking the mustard with the garlic, sugar, vinegar and seasoning, then whisk in the oil until you have a glossy emulsion. Pour half over the warm potatoes, bacon and croûtons, and toss well.

Put the eggs in a pan of cold water, bring to the boil and cook for 4 minutes. Drain and run the eggs under cold water to stop the cooking, then peel the eggs and set aside.

Add the Comté cheese, cherry tomatoes, chopped chives and lettuce to the serving bowl with the potatoes and toss everything together.

Halve the eggs and place on top of the salad. Serve immediately, drizzled with extra dressing.

SALADE MÊLÉE

12–16 (depending on thickness) asparagus spears, white and green

120 g/4 oz. green beans

1 large carrot, cut into matchsticks

200 g/7 oz. chèvre goat's cheese rounds

1 egg, beaten

50 g/⅔ cup dried breadcrumbs

vegetable oil, to fry

90 g/3½ oz. mixed baby salad leaves, such as baby beetroot/beet and lamb's lettuce

1 radicchio, torn

50 g/⅓ cup walnuts

2 tablespoons cider vinegar

a pinch of sugar

4 tablespoons extra virgin olive oil

sea salt and ground black pepper

SERVES 2

This is a mixed salad by any other name, so anything goes! I am particularly fond of the salads at Maurice et Mauricette in the Swiss village in the Valais that I have been visiting with my family for nearly 30 years. The restaurant used to be called Bernard after its patron, André-Bernard Gross, a local ski-touring god and mountain-climbing legend, who looked like a rock star with flowing locks, Cuban heels and a penchant for lacy (ladies) underwear that you could see peeking out from the top of his leather trousers. A legend no doubt, but since M&M have taken over this lovely mountain spot, the food has become what it is famous for! (Opposite.)

Plunge the asparagus and beans into boiling water for a couple of minutes then drain and refresh under cold water. Toss with the carrot.

Dip each round of goat's cheese in the beaten egg then coat in the breadcrumbs. Heat a good layer of oil in a non-stick frying pan/skillet and fry the cheese until golden on both sides. Drain on paper towels.

Mix the vegetables with the leaves and divide between two plates. Scatter with the walnuts. Whisk the vinegar with salt, pepper and a pinch of sugar, then gradually whisk in the oil. Pour over the salads then top with the fried cheese.

COBB SALAD

a little oil, to fry

8 slices of streaky/fatty bacon

3 eggs

½ iceberg lettuce, chopped

1 romain lettuce, chopped

2 green chicory heads, chopped

3 ripe vine tomatoes, chopped

250 g/9 oz. cooked chicken, chopped

1 large ripe avocado, peeled, stoned/pitted and chopped

150 g/5 oz. Roquefort cheese, crumbled

a small bunch of fresh chives, chopped

FOR THE DRESSING

50 ml/scant ¼ cup red wine vinegar

a squeeze of lemon juice

1 garlic clove, crushed

a good pinch of sugar

a dash of Worcestershire sauce

a pinch of English mustard powder

75 ml/scant ⅓ cup extra virgin olive oil

50 ml/scant ¼ cup olive oil

SERVES 6

The ultimate in American garden salads, this is the stateside version of a salade mêlée. Unlike its European mixed-salad counterparts, there is a set list of ingredients for a cobb salad, which have to be strictly adhered to.

Heat a little oil in a pan and fry the bacon until crisp. Set aside.

Cook the eggs in boiling water for 6–8 minutes then drain and cool under cold running water.

Put the salad leaves in a serving bowl. Peel and chop the eggs and scatter over the top. Add the chopped tomatoes, chicken and avocado.

Tear up the bacon and scatter on top, along with the crumbled cheese and chopped chives.

Whisk everything but the oils together for the dressing, then gradually whisk in the oils. You can add a splash of water if it is too thick.

Pour the dressing over the salad and serve at once.

SALADE MONTAGNARDE

500 ml/2 cups chicken stock
350 g/heaping 1¾ cups Puy lentils
5 fresh thyme sprigs
oil, to fry
200 g/7 oz. smoked bacon lardons
2 tablespoons red wine vinegar
a pinch of sugar
1 fat garlic clove, crushed
2 teaspoons Dijon mustard
3 tablespoons extra virgin olive oil
1 sweet onion, thinly sliced
sea salt and ground black pepper

SERVES 4

Here is a dish that has many names and varying ingredients, depending on where you are in the Alps, unsurprising as its name means 'salad of the mountain dwellers'. I have based mine on a fantastic lunch I had in Méribel, where five of us crowded around a tiny terrace table eating poulet frite and salade montagnarde, washed down with lots of rosé. (Pictured opposite.)

Bring the stock to the boil, then tip in the lentils and thyme and plenty of seasoning. Simmer for 15–20 minutes until the lentils are tender.

Meanwhile, heat a pan with a little oil and fry the lardons until golden and crisp. Remove with a slotted spoon and reserve the fat.

Whisk the vinegar with a pinch of sugar, some salt and pepper, the garlic and mustard. Gradually whisk in the oil, then whisk in the reserved bacon fat.

Drain the lentils and toss with the dressing and the lardons. Tip onto a serving plate and scatter with the onion, then serve.

APPENZELLER FRITTERS

250 ml/generous 1 cup whole/full-fat milk
200 g/7 oz. Appenzeller cheese, grated
200 ml/scant 1 cup beer
250 g/1¾ cups plus 2 tablespoons plain/all-purpose flour
1 teaspoon baking powder
4 eggs
vegetable oil, to fry
sea salt, to sprinkle

large disposable piping/pastry bag

SERVES 8 AS A SNACK WITH BEER

I came across the idea for these fritters in a fabulously 1970s book on Swiss food. I couldn't resist trying them out, as I am a sucker for anything that is deep-fried. A bit of tweaking later, and what we have is perhaps the most wonderful fried bar snack I have ever eaten. Golden and crunchy on the outside it has a soft, cheesy centre. Plan on having a lighter supper after eating these, as you won't be able to stop at just one.

Heat the milk to just below boiling point, then add the grated cheese. Remove from the heat and allow the hot milk to melt the cheese.

Blend the beer with the flour and baking powder until smooth. Beat the eggs in, one at a time, then stir into the cheese mixture. You should have a lovely thick batter. If it is still a bit thin you can add a little more flour.

Pour into a large piping/pastry bag. Leave to stand for 10 minutes.

Heat 5 cm/2 in. oil in a pan to 180°C (350°F). Snip the end of the bag and then pipe the cheese mixture into the oil in concentric circles like a snail shell. Allow to fry until golden and puffed up.

Remove with a slotted spoon and drain on paper towels. Serve immediately, sprinkled with sea salt.

PARMESAN AND RICOTTA CHEESECAKE

125 g/4 oz. oatcakes

75 g/3 oz. digestive biscuits/graham crackers

25 g/scant ¼ cup walnuts

100 g/1 cup minus 1 tablespoon unsalted butter, melted

300 g/1⅓ cups cream cheese

300 g/1⅓ cups ricotta cheese

150 g/2¼ cups freshly grated Parmesan

4 eggs

a small bunch of fresh chives, chopped

ground black pepper

20-cm/8-in. loose-bottomed or springform cake pan, greased

SERVES 8 HUNGRY PEOPLE

I confess that I don't really understand cheesecake as a dessert – not that I dislike it, it just doesn't fill me with the joy that many seem to get. A savoury cheesecake, on the other hand, now that is something I can really get behind. As well as making a first-class lunch with salad, this also makes a different and exciting end to a meal – a cheese course in different form. (Opposite.)

Whiz the oatcakes, digestive biscuits/graham crackers and walnuts to fine crumbs. Stir with the melted butter so that it resembles wet sand.

Press the crumbs into the base of the pan, and push them so they come a little way up the side of the pan. Chill for at least 30 minutes.

Preheat the oven to 150°C (300°F) Gas 2.

Beat the cream cheese, ricotta and Parmesan together until smooth, then beat in the eggs and chives. Season with plenty of black pepper. Pour onto the base, then bake for 50 minutes–1 hour until set but with a slight wobble in the centre. Cool in the pan before turning out.

BRISOLÉE

1 kg/2¼ lb. raw chestnuts in their shells

TO SERVE

dry cured meats, such as saucisson sec, viande séchée, bresaola

a mixture of alpine cheeses, such as tomme, Gruyère, raclette, Appenzeller

fruit, such as grapes or pear slices

fresh rye bread

SERVES 4

This is not so much of a recipe as a collection of the finest ingredients. Chestnuts are one of autumn and winter's seasonal delights, and showcasing them simply roasted as the main part of a meal is often the way in the mountains. If you use an open fire, they will have an amazing smoky flavour, but not to worry if you just have your trusty oven.

Split or skewer the chestnuts to help make them easier to peel. Roast the chestnuts over the embers of a fire in a cast-iron pan (preferably a chestnut pan with holes to allow the heat to be evenly distributed). Cook until the chestnuts are slightly blackened and you can smell the lovely aroma.

Alternatively, preheat the grill/broiler to high, or the oven to 230°C (450°F) Gas 8, and grill/broil or roast the chestnuts, turning them regularly, until tender.

Allow to cool a little, then peel and serve with the meats, cheese, fruit and bread.

TIROLER GRÖSTL

250 g/9 oz. smoked bacon, chopped
a little oil, to fry
1 onion, thinly sliced
500 g/1lb. 2oz. potatoes, boiled and
cut into pieces
1 teaspoon caraway seeds
1 teaspoon smoked sweet paprika
1 teaspoon smoked hot paprika
4 eggs
freshly chopped parsley, to garnish
sea salt and ground black pepper

SERVES 4

Here is a fabulous Tyrolean fry-up that produces a 'set you up for the day' kind of breakfast. It works equally well as an energy-fuelling lunch or a comforting supper after a long, hard day. (Pictured opposite.)

Fry the bacon in a little oil in a frying pan/skillet until crisp. Remove with a slotted spoon and set aside, then add the onion to the pan and fry for 15 minutes until golden and softened. Remove the onion and add to the bacon.

Add a little more oil to the pan and tip in the potatoes. Allow to cook, without moving, until golden brown underneath, then turn. Once golden all over, return the onion and bacon to the pan and add the caraway, paprika and plenty of seasoning. Fry together for a few minutes while you cook the eggs.

Heat a layer of oil in a second frying pan/skillet and fry the eggs for 1–2 minutes until cooked to your liking.

Serve the hash with the eggs on top and a scattering of parsley.

TROUT À LA MEUNIÈRE

4 trout fillets
plain/all-purpose flour, seasoned, to dust
olive oil, to fry
30 g/2 tablespoons unsalted butter
freshly squeezed juice of 1 lemon
3 tablespoons capers, drained and rinsed
a handful of fresh flat leaf parsley, finely chopped
sea salt and ground black pepper

SERVES 4

There is a surprising amount of fish in the mountains, such as fera and perch from the deep, cold lakes. These fish don't often find their way to the UK or US, and even when they do some people seem to be suspicious of freshwater fish, fearing that they may taste muddy, which they never should. This classic dish is delicious with rainbow or brown trout, but you could also make it with sea trout when it is in season. (Pictured on page 83.)

Dust the fish fillets in seasoned flour, shaking off any excess. Heat a layer of oil in a non-stick frying pan/skillet and fry the fish until golden brown on both sides and just cooked through. Remove from the pan and set aside.

Add the butter to the pan and allow to foam and start to become brown and nutty.

Stir in the lemon, capers and parsley and serve immediately with the fish.

POACHED SALMON WITH GREEN MAYONNAISE

600 ml/generous 2½ cups white wine

1 litre/4⅓ cups water

2 bay leaves

4 fresh thyme sprigs

5 fresh tarragon sprigs

a handful of fresh parsley stalks

2 shallots, halved

1 carrot, sliced

1.5 kg/3¾ lb. salmon, trout or sea trout, gutted and scaled

FOR THE MAYONNAISE

2 egg yolks

1 tablespoon white wine vinegar

400 ml/1¾ cups light mild oil, such as groundnut/peanut oil

150 ml/scant ⅔ cup light olive oil

50 ml/scant ¼ cup extra virgin olive oil

a good squeeze of lemon juice

2 tablespoons each freshly chopped flat leaf parsley and chives

1 tablespoon freshly chopped tarragon

sea salt

SERVES 6-8

A whole poached salmon is a thing of beauty and surprisingly simple to cook. The mayonnaise is based on one of my favourite dressings, green goddess, which is packed full of luscious herbs. Even during the depths of winter snow in the mountains there are days of glorious sunshine, and this is a dish for just such a day.

Put the wine and water in a large pan or roasting pan that is big enough for the fish to fit in. Tie the bay leaves, thyme, tarragon and parsley together with a piece of cook's string and add to the pan with the shallots and carrot.

Cover and bring to the boil then simmer gently for 20-30 minutes. Butter a large piece of muslin/cheesecloth and wrap the fish in it. This is to make it easy to lift it out of the poaching liquid. Add the fish to the stock, cover and simmer very gently for 20-25 minutes.

Meanwhile, make the mayonnaise. Put the yolks in a bowl with the vinegar and a good pinch of sea salt. Gradually whisk in the neutral oil, then the light olive oil and finally the extra virgin olive oil until you have a thick, glossy mayonnaise. Add lemon juice to taste and all the herbs.

Allow the fish to cool for 10 minutes in the stock, then carefully remove it and put on a serving dish. Peel back the skin and serve with the mayonnaise and baby new potatoes.

RÖSTI

600 g/1 lb. 5 oz. floury potatoes, such as Maris Piper/Yukon Gold

50 g/3½ tablespoons unsalted butter, melted

a little oil, to fry

SERVES 2-3

I think I may be suffering from an addiction to rösti. I just can't get enough of the simplicity of buttery fried potato, it is so comforting. I love them plain, with dollops of sour cream and apple sauce. They are like the little Jewish latkes my husband's family serve at any available opportunity, and which never last for more than a few moments on the plate, but I also adore rösti for lunch, with cured meats and salamis, little slices of nutty cheese and lots and lots of cornichons. (Pictured opposite.)

Coarsely grate the potatoes into a bowl then pour over a kettleful of boiling water and leave to stand for a minute or two. Drain, then, once cool enough to handle, squeeze out as much water as you can using paper towels. Tip into a bowl and toss with the melted butter.

Take a heavy-based frying pan/skillet (or several little ones). Heat a little oil in the bottom. Divide the grated potato between the pans and press down. Cook very gently for 6-8 minutes, loosening the rösti after a couple of minutes, so that it doesn't stick, until golden brown on the bottom.

Flip out carefully onto a plate and heat the rest of the butter and oil in the pan(s). Slide the rösti(s) back in, top-side down, and continue to cook for a further 6-8 minutes over a very low heat.

CHICKEN LIVER PARFAIT

350 g/3 sticks unsalted butter
500 g/1lb. 2oz. chicken livers, trimmed
2 tablespoons brandy
freshly grated nutmeg
a pinch of ground allspice
sea salt and ground black pepper

600-ml/2½-cup dish

SERVES 8–10

Nothing beats a really rich and smooth chicken liver parfait. There are two ways of making parfait, but this version is by far the simplest and quickest. Although it doesn't have quite the amazing pink colour of a slow-cooked bain-marie parfait, its taste is just as good. (Pictured opposite.)

Melt 200 g/1¾ sticks of the butter in a pan, then leave to cool. Brush the dish with a little of the melted butter and set aside.

Melt 50 g/3½ tablespoons of the butter in another pan, season the livers and fry them over a medium-high heat until brown on each side, but still pink in the middle. Add the brandy and flambé by carefully lighting with a match or flame to burn off the excess alcohol, then tip into a food processor.

Gradually add the cooled melted butter, whizzing all the time, until you have a smooth mixture. Season with some nutmeg, allspice and plenty of salt and pepper. Strain into the greased dish. Chill in the fridge for 30 minutes.

Melt the remaining 100 g/7 tablespoons of butter then pour off just the clear butter and discard any milk solids at the bottom of the pan. Pour over the parfait and chill until set. Serve with brioche toasts and fruit jelly.

PORK RILLETTES

1.5 kg/3¼ lb. piece boneless fatty pork belly
12 juniper berries, crushed
3 bay leaves
10 black peppercorns
a handful of fresh thyme sprigs
3 garlic cloves, peeled
sea salt

FOR THE PICKLED RED ONION
2 red onions, thinly sliced
75 ml/scant ⅓ cup distilled malt vinegar
30 g/2½ tablespoons caster/superfine sugar
1 star anise
5 peppercorns

SERVES 8

A simple classic, slow-cooked pork belly needs very little adornment. My accompanying little pickle cuts through the meatiness of the pork, lifting it and bringing out its sweet flavour, although it is just as delicious with cornichons and pickled baby onions. (Pictured on page 89.)

Preheat the oven to 150°C (300°F) Gas 2.

Put the pork in a deep roasting pan with the remaining ingredients and a good handful of sea salt. Pour over 350 ml/1½ cups water and cover with foil. Cook for 3–4 hours until completely tender and falling apart.

Remove the meat from the pan and strain the pan juices into a jug/pitcher, then discard the herbs and spices. Shred the meat with two forks, discarding the skin (unless you want to turn up the oven and make it into crackling), then pack into small sterilized jars. Pour over the reserved liquid and allow to cool. Chill for at least 30 minutes.

To make the pickled red onion, put the onions in a bowl. Heat the vinegar in a small pan with the sugar and spices, until the sugar has dissolved. Pour the hot liquid over the onion and leave to cool.

Bring the rillettes to room temperature before serving with the pickled red onion, cornichons and toast.

TERRINE OF VENISON AND RABBIT

30 g/2 tablespoons butter, plus extra for greasing

2 banana shallots, finely chopped

50 ml/scant ¼ cup brandy

650 g/1lb. 7oz. boneless rabbit meat, diced

450 g/1 lb. venison haunch, diced

200 g/7 oz. bacon lardons

finely grated zest of 1 lemon

1 teaspoon ground mace

½ teaspoon ground allspice

leaves from 5 fresh thyme sprigs

a handful of freshly chopped flat leaf parsley

1 egg, beaten

25 slices pancetta or streaky/fatty bacon

4 bay leaves

sea salt and ground black pepper

1.3-kg/3-lb terrine dish or loaf pan

SERVES 6

Wild deer and rabbit are staples of the mountains and this terrine is very versatile, from a rustic lunch with crusty bread and pickles to a more glamorous appetizer for dinner with little toasts.

Melt the butter in a pan and gently fry the shallots for 10 minutes until lovely and softened. Add the brandy and bubble away for a minute, then remove from the heat and allow to cool.

Put half the rabbit and venison in a food processor and whiz until minced/ground. Alternatively, use a mincer attachment on a stand mixer, if you have one. Tip into a bowl with the rest of the diced meat. Mince the bacon lardons and add to the bowl.

Add the lemon zest, spices, herbs, egg and plenty of salt and pepper to the bowl, and mix together using your hands. Fry a little of the mixture in a pan in a little oil and taste to check the seasoning; adjust if necessary.

Put the bay leaves along the bottom of the terrine dish. With the back of a knife, stretch the pancetta or bacon slices to twice their length and use them to line the terrine dish or loaf pan, reserving a couple of slices for the top. Overlap the pancetta slightly to make sure there are no gaps and leave the ends overhanging the edges of the dish.

Spoon the filling evenly into the lined dish and press down. Fold the overhanging pancetta over the top to enclose the filling. Use the reserved extra slices to make sure the top is fully covered. Place in the fridge to chill for a couple of hours.

Preheat the oven to 170°C (340°F) Gas 3½.

Cover the terrine with a buttered sheet of foil. If you have a lid for your terrine dish, put it on the top. Put the dish into a deep roasting pan and pour boiling water into the pan so that it comes about halfway up the side of the terrine dish or loaf pan.

Transfer to the preheated oven and cook for about 1¼ hours, until the juices run clear when the terrine is pierced in the centre with a skewer.

Remove from the oven and the roasting pan, then leave to cool for 1 hour.

Leave the terrine in its dish and chill it overnight in the fridge, then turn out and slice to serve.

STEAK TARTARE

400 g/14 oz. beef fillet/tenderloin
1 banana shallot (about 80 g/3¼ oz.),
very finely diced
80 g/3¼ oz. gherkins, chopped
4 teaspoons capers, drained and rinsed
2 egg yolks, very fresh
Worcestershire sauce and Tabasco, to taste
sea salt and ground black pepper

SERVES 2

An odd choice for a mountain recipe perhaps, but yet this is something that appears all over the Alps on many menus, so, to me, it has become part of Alpine cuisine. Make sure you use the best-quality steak you can afford, as it will really make a difference to the flavour of this dish.

Finely chop the steak, as fine as you can but not minced/ground. Add the shallot, gherkins and capers, and season well.

Divide in half and shape into neat mounds on two plates. Make a hollow in the centre and place a egg yolk in each. Serve with melba toast. Allow each person to season their tartar with their own Worcestershire sauce and Tabasco.

MOUNTAIN MEATS

BUFFALO BURGER

500 g/1lb. 2oz. minced/ground buffalo

100 g/3¾ oz. streaky/fatty bacon, finely chopped

2 garlic cloves

1 tablespoon freshly chopped parsley

1 teaspoon freshly chopped sage

50 g/2 oz. blue cheese

a little vegetable oil, to fry

4 burger buns, halved

2 tablespoons mayonnaise

½ red onion, sliced into rings

soft green lettuce

1 large vine tomato, sliced

SERVES 4

A good burger on a menu is a hard thing to pass over, such is the lure of the intensely meaty, juicy patty. In the mountains of the US and Canada, they often use buffalo meat instead of beef, which has a more intense flavour. Herds of buffalo are now also bred in the UK, so buffalo meat (like buffalo mozzarella) is readily available, but you can always make these with beef if you prefer.

In a bowl, mix the minced/ground meat, bacon, garlic and herbs together using your hands. Season well and divide into 4. Flatten each piece and put a quarter of the cheese in the centre, then wrap the meat around it to enclose it. Flatten into a patty.

Preheat the oven to 200°C (400°F) Gas 6. Heat a little vegetable oil in an ovenproof frying pan or griddle over a medium-high heat and fry the burgers for 2–3 minutes on each side until browned. Transfer the pan to the oven and cook for 4–5 minutes.

Put on a warm plate to rest. Put the pan back over a medium-high heat and toast the cut sides of the burger buns in the pan. Spread them with mayonnaise and add the burgers topped with the onion, lettuce and tomato, and serve.

MEATLOAF

a knob of unsalted butter, plus extra for greasing

2 tablespoons olive oil

1 onion, finely chopped

1 garlic clove, crushed

1 green pepper/bell pepper, deseeded and finely chopped

500 g/1lb. 2oz. minced/ground beef

100 g/3¾ oz. smoked streaky/fatty bacon, finely chopped

50 g/1 cup brown fresh breadcrumbs

1 tablespoon tomato ketchup, plus extra to serve

1 tablespoon Worcestershire sauce

a few shakes of Tabasco, to taste

1 UK large/US extra-large egg

1 tablespoon freshly chopped oregano

50 g/½ scant cup grated Cheddar cheese

50 g/½ cup crumbled blue cheese

sea salt and ground black pepper

1.5-litre/6½-cup ovenproof dish, greased

SERVES 4–6

A bit of a 1970s throwback perhaps, but there is something about a meatloaf that takes me back to my childhood. It's an American classic that deserves to be revived. Serve it with garlic bread.

Heat the oven to 180°C (350°F) Gas 4.

Melt the butter and oil in a pan and gently fry the onion for 10 minutes, then add the garlic and green pepper/bell pepper and fry for 5 minutes more. Tip into a bowl and allow to cool, then add the beef, bacon, breadcrumbs, ketchup, Worcestershire sauce and Tabasco.

Mix well, then add the egg, oregano and half the cheeses, and season well. Spoon into the dish and press down.

Cover with buttered foil and bake in the preheated oven for 1 hour. There will be lots of juices, but these juices are delicious so don't throw them away; you can always spoon off a little of the fat if you like.

Remove from the oven and turn the oven up to 220°C (425°F) Gas 7.

Remove the foil and sprinkle with the remaining cheese. Bake for 10 minutes until the cheese is melted and bubbling. Serve in slices with extra ketchup.

STICKY BOURBON RIBS

Tangy, sweet and sticky, these ribs hit the spot every time. The key is to cook them low and slow with plenty of marinade, only lifting the cover to let them get sticky towards the very end.

Whiz the tomatoes with the remaining ingredients, except the ribs, until smooth. Pour over the ribs in a non-metallic container. Cover and marinate overnight in the fridge.

Preheat the oven to 150°C (300°F) Gas 2.

Transfer the ribs to a roasting pan, reserving any spare marinade. Cover with foil and roast for 3–3½ hours, basting occasionally, until tender. Pour off any marinade into a pan and add any reserved marinade. Place over a medium heat and bubble until thick and glossy.

Increase the oven to 200°C (400°F) Gas 6. Pour over the thickened glaze and return the ribs to the oven for 20–25 minutes until sticky.

400 g/14 oz. can tomatoes
4 garlic cloves, crushed
100 g/½ cup soft light brown sugar
75 ml/5 tablespoons maple syrup
150 ml/scant ⅔ cup barbecue sauce
150 ml/scant ⅔ cup tomato sauce
100 ml/scant ½ cup bourbon
50 ml/scant ¼ cup cider vinegar
2 tablespoons black treacle/molasses
3 tablespoons soy sauce
2 tablespoons Worcestershire sauce
2 kg/4½ lb. baby back or spare ribs

SERVES 4

SCHNITZEL WITH WARM POTATO SALAD

1 small white loaf, preferably 1 or
2 days old

4 veal escalopes, preferably British
rose veal, about 130 g/4½ oz. each

2 tablespoons plain/all-purpose flour

1 UK large/US extra-large egg, beaten

1 tablespoon double/heavy cream

vegetable oil, to fry

30 g/2 tablespoons unsalted butter

sea salt and ground black pepper

lemon wedges, to serve

FOR THE POTATO SALAD

750 g/1 lb. 10 oz. waxy new potatoes,
halved

1 red onion, thinly sliced

3 tablespoons white wine vinegar

1 tablespoon Dijon mustard

3 tablespoons mayonnaise

2 tablespoons extra virgin olive oil

2 tablespoons crème fraîche

a pinch of caster/superfine sugar

12 cocktail gherkins, finely chopped

1 tablespoon gherkin liquid

a few sprigs of fresh tarragon,
finely chopped

a small bunch of fresh flat leaf parsley,
leaves finely chopped

SERVES 4

Traditionally made with veal, schnitzel is equally delicious when made with pork or even chicken. A schnitzel should be lovely and thin with a crisp, golden casing of crumbs. Here they are served with a classic German potato salad that has a tang of vinegar and pickles to offset the creamy dressing.

Preheat the oven to 110°C (225°F) Gas ¼.

Remove and discard the crusts from the loaf and whiz it in a food processor or blender to form coarse crumbs. Spread the crumbs onto a baking sheet and cook in the preheated the oven for about an hour to dry out slowly – start checking them after 30 minutes. Once dry, whiz again to make fine crumbs. You can keep any you don't use in an airtight container for several weeks.

Put the escalopes between two pieces of baking parchment or clingfilm/plastic wrap and bash with a meat tenderizer or rolling pin until they are as thin as possible, without tearing the meat.

For the potato salad, put the potatoes in a pan of cold salted water and bring to the boil, then simmer for 15 minutes until just tender.

Meanwhile, put the onion in a bowl with the vinegar. When the potatoes are cooked, drain them and mix with all the remaining potato salad ingredients, including the onion and vinegar. Season well and set aside.

Season the flour with plenty of salt and pepper and put in a shallow dish. Beat the egg with the cream and put in a second dish. Put 150 g/3 cups of the crumbs in a third dish (or more, if you need to).

Heat a good layer of oil in a large non-stick frying pan/skillet. Dip each of the escalopes into the flour, shaking off any excess, then coat in the beaten egg and finally the breadcrumbs. Make sure the escalopes are completely coated.

Add the butter to the pan, and once it is melted and foaming, add the escalopes. Fry for 1–2 minutes on each side until golden. You may need to cook them one or two at a time, depending on the size of your pan.

Serve immediately with lemon wedges and the warm potato salad.

SAUSAGE AND CHOUCROUTE

Up until recently I had never tried making choucroute, deeming the good-quality stuff you get in jars and packs being as good as any I could make – but I was wrong. Home-made choucroute, or sauerkraut, has a much subtler delicate flavour that is vastly superior. This recipe is for choucroute crue (raw) which is completely delicious, but I also tried my hand at choucroute garnie, the traditional Alsatian dish, where it is served hot, fried up with pork fat, white wine and often onions, apples and spices.

1 white cabbage, cored
1½ tablespoons sea salt
1 tablespoon caraway seeds
1 large curl of sausage or 12 meaty sausages, such as saucisse de veau or bratwurst
plenty of hot mustard, to serve

large sterilized jar with lid

SERVES 6

Finely slice the cabbage into thin shreds about 5 cm/2 in. long. Put in a large bowl and sprinkle over the salt. Work the salt in with your fingers, until the cabbage becomes limp and a little watery. Add the caraway seeds and mix well.

Spoon the cabbage into the sterilized jar, packing it down. You then want to weight the cabbage down in the jar as much as possible. Fill a smaller jar with clean stones, marbles or coins and put inside the large jar. Cover the jar with a piece of muslin/cheesecloth and secure with an elastic/rubber band. You don't want to seal the jar properly, as you need the air to get in to get the fermentation process started.

Leave for 24 hours, pressing down occasionally so that all the cabbage is submerged in the liquid. If there isn't quite enough liquid after 24 hours, add a little water to help the process along.

You then want to leave it in a cool, dark place for 3–10 days. Scoop off any white foam that gathers on the top. Start tasting after 3 days and continue to ferment until you are happy with the taste. At this point, you can seal the jar and transfer it to the fridge. It will keep in the fridge for a couple of months.

Grill your sausages until golden all over and serve with the sauerkraut and lots of mustard.

MORTEAU SAUSAGE AND CREAMY LENTILS

2 large Morteau sausages
750 ml/3¼ cups chicken stock
400 g/heaping 2 cups Puy lentils
2 tablespoons olive oil
2 shallots, thinly sliced
100 ml/scant ½ cup crème fraîche
3 tablespoons double/heavy cream
1 tablespoon Dijon mustard, plus extra
to serve
a good squeeze of lemon juice
a large handful of freshly chopped herbs,
such as parsley, tarragon, chervil

SERVES 6

Friends of mine who live in the Jura region in France introduced me to this very special smoked sausage, which is made in the Jura mountains from pigs that are fattened traditionally. The sausages are smoked for 48 hours in special chimneys over sawdust, pine and juniper, which gives them a strong and distinctive flavour. Once they are cooked, the slices of sausage are juicy, rich and wonderful.

Bring a large pan of water to the boil and add the sausages. Cover and simmer gently for about 30 minutes.

In a separate pan, bring the stock to the boil and add the lentils. Simmer for 15–20 minutes until tender.

Meanwhile, heat the oil in a frying pan/skillet and gently fry the shallots for 10 minutes.

As soon as the lentils are cooked, tip them into the pan with the shallots, then add the remaining ingredients. Toss everything together until well mixed and coated.

Drain and thickly slice the sausage, and serve on top of the creamy lentils with lots of extra mustard.

CONFIT DUCK

Whenever I make confit duck I always wonder why I don't make it more often. Confit means to preserve (usually in its own fat) in French, and that is what makes this such a great dish. Once you have gone through the fairly simple process of making it, you have this wonderful slow-cooked, tender duck at your fingertips to use at a moment's notice.

6 UK large/US extra-large
duck legs

160 g/5½ oz. flaky sea salt

1 kg/2¼ lb. duck or goose fat

1 garlic bulb, cloves separated
and bruised

20 black peppercorns

a handful of fresh thyme sprigs

3 bay leaves

SERVES 6

Rub the duck legs with salt then put in a non-metallic container and scatter over the rest of the salt. Put in the fridge for 24 hours.

Preheat the oven to 140°C (275°F) Gas 1.

Brush the salt off the duck legs with paper towels. Put the fat in a deep ovenproof dish or roasting pan and place in the oven to melt. Add the rest of the ingredients and the duck legs.

Cover with foil and cook for 2½ hours until the duck legs are really tender.

Remove from the oven and leave to cool in the fat. At this point, you can transfer the legs to a container and strain over the cooled fat to completely cover, then chill for up to 4–5 weeks in the fridge.

When you are ready to eat them, take them out of the fridge and leave to stand at room temperature for 1 hour. Remove as many legs as you want and scrape off any excess fat.

Preheat the oven to 220°C (425°F) Gas 7.

Put the legs on a baking sheet, skin-side down, and roast for 20–25 minutes until the skin is crisp.

KIDNEYS WITH CREAM AND MUSTARD

500 g/1lb. 2oz. calves' kidneys, cleaned and trimmed and cut into large bite-sized pieces

plain/all-purpose flour for dusting

50 g/3½ tablespoons unsalted butter

a little olive oil

50 g/2 oz. smoked bacon lardons

1 shallot, thinly sliced

100 ml/scant ½ cup Madeira

100 ml/scant ½ cup chicken stock

2 tablespoons Dijon mustard

50 ml/scant ¼ cup double/heavy cream

a handful of fresh flat leaf parsley, finely chopped

sea salt and ground black pepper

SERVES 4

The best dishes are ones that remind you of a time or place. Kidneys are not something I often order, but I first had ones like these at the very top of a mountain. They came bubbling in their own little pan, turning heads as the smell wafted over the terrace. I barely got a look in as the rest of the group dived in with hunks of bread, but the kidneys were so wonderfully tender and delicious that I now order them on nearly every visit.

Dust the kidney pieces in the flour and season well. Melt just over half the butter in a frying pan/skillet and, when it starts to foam, add the kidneys and fry for 1–2 minutes, then flip them over. You want them to form a lovely golden crust. Remove from the pan and set aside.

Add the rest of the butter to the pan with the oil and fry the lardons until starting to crisp.

Add the shallot and fry until golden and soft. Return the kidneys to the pan and pour in the Madeira. Bubble for a minute or two, then add the stock and mustard. Simmer together for a few seconds before sloshing in the cream.

Bring back to a simmer, season and serve immediately with creamy mash or on toasted sourdough bread, scattered with parsley.

BLANQUETTE D'AGNEAU

1 kg/2¼ lb. diced lamb leg or neck

1.5 litres/6½ cups chicken stock

1 bouquet garni (fresh thyme, parsley, bay leaves, tied in a bunch)

200 g/7 oz. shallots, peeled

250 g/9 oz. Chantenay carrots

50 g/3½ tablespoons unsalted butter

50 g/heaping ⅓ cup plain/all-purpose flour

2 egg yolks, beaten

75 ml/scant ⅓ cup double/heavy cream

sea salt and ground black pepper

a squeeze of lemon juice

SERVES 4

A comforting, almost nursery-food dish, blanquette d'agneau is simple and straightforward, and, as the name would suggest, it is wrapped in a blanket of creamy sauce. It's a dish for snowy, wind-blown days.

Season the lamb and put it in a pan with the stock and bouquet garni. Bring to the boil, then turn down to a simmer and cook for 45 minutes, then add the shallots and carrots, and cook for a further 45 minutes until the lamb is tender. Strain off the stock and keep the meat and veggies warm.

Melt the butter in a pan and add the flour, cook for a minute or so until it

smells nutty, then gradually add about 600 ml/2½ cups of the reserved stock, stirring until you have a smooth sauce.

Add the egg yolks to the sauce and cook over a low heat, without boiling, until thickened. Add the cream and plenty of seasoning, and then the lemon juice.

Serve the lamb and veggies with the sauce spooned over the top.

olive oil, to fry

4 pieces veal shin, cut through the bone with the marrow, about 350 g/12 oz. each

4 tablespoons plain/all-purpose flour

50 g/3½ tablespoons butter

1 onion, finely chopped

1 carrot, finely chopped

2 celery sticks, finely chopped

6 garlic cloves, crushed

finely grated zest of 1 lemon

leaves from 6 fresh thyme sprigs

200 ml/scant 1 cup white wine

250 ml/generous 1 cup chicken stock

FOR THE RISOTTO

2 tablespoons olive oil

2 banana shallots, thinly sliced

300 g/heaping 1½ cups Arborio risotto rice

175 ml/scant ¾ cup white wine

a pinch of saffron strands, soaked in 1 tablespoon hot water

1 litre/4⅓ cups hot chicken stock

30 g/scant 1 cup freshly grated Parmesan

a good knob/pat of butter

FOR THE GREMOLATA

finely grated zest of 1 lemon

1 garlic clove, crushed

a small handful of fresh flat leaf parsley, finely chopped

SERVES 4

OSSO BUCCO WITH RISOTTO

I had to include this dish because it is one of my father's all-time favourites. Although not strictly speaking from the mountains, this dish, for me, sums up all that is good about winter cooking. The name of this dish (osso, meaning 'bone' and bucco meaning 'hole') refers to the veal shank with its central hole filled with the all-important marrow, which thickens the dish and gives it a lovely rich flavour. You will probably need to go to the butcher to get the meat for this dish, but is well worth the trip. (Opposite.)

Heat the olive oil in a heavy-based flameproof casserole large enough to fit all the veal in single layer. Dust the veal in the flour and season well, then brown all over and set aside.

Add a little more oil to the pan and fry the onion, carrot and celery for about 10 minutes until softened. Add the garlic, lemon zest and thyme and return the browned veal. Slosh in the wine and bubble away for a minute or so, then add the stock. Bring to a simmer, cover and cook very gently for 1½ hours.

Remove the lid and simmer for a further 30 minutes to reduce the sauce slightly. The veal should be lovely and tender. In the final 30 minutes make the risotto.

Heat the oil in a pan and fry the shallots until softened. Add the risotto rice and stir over a medium heat for a minute or so. Add the wine and stir until absorbed.

Add the saffron and its water, and then add the hot stock, a ladleful at a time, stirring until each addition is absorbed before adding the next.

Once it is just tender, add another good ladleful of stock, the Parmesan and butter. Stir, then remove from the heat, cover and leave to stand for 5 minutes.

Mix all the ingredients together for the gremolata. Serve the osso bucco on top of the risotto and sprinkle with the gremolata.

45 g/3 tablespoons unsalted butter

1 tablespoon olive oil

1 large onion, very thinly sliced

450 g/1 lb. leftover roast meat, chopped

800 g/1¾ lb. potatoes, cut into cubes

2 cooking apples, peeled, cored and sliced

300 ml/1¼ cups chicken stock or leftover gravy mixed with boiling water

100 g/2 cups fresh breadcrumbs

sea salt and ground black pepper

2.5-litre/11-cup ovenproof dish

SERVES 4

HUNTSMAN'S PIE

I think that sometimes I cook extra just so that I can have leftovers to play with in the next few days. This dish is so easily adaptable to whatever meat you might have left from your Sunday roast.

Preheat the oven to 160°C (325°F) Gas 3.

Melt 15 g/1 tablespoon of the butter with the oil in a pan and gently fry the onion for 10 minutes until softened. Let cool.

Layer the meat, potatoes, fried onion and apples in the ovenproof dish, and season each layer. Bring the stock to a simmer and pour over the dish.

Scatter with the breadcrumbs and dot all over with the remaining butter.

Bake in the preheated oven for 1 hour until golden and crispy on top.

VENISON FILLETS WITH BRANDY SAUCE

olive oil to fry and coat
50 g/3½ tablespoons unsalted butter
2 shallots, finely chopped
2 garlic cloves, crushed
150 g/2½ cups button mushrooms, sliced
4 tablespoons brandy
100 ml/scant ½ cup beef stock
75 ml/5 tablespoons double/heavy cream
800 g/1¾ lb. venison fillet/tenderloin
1 tablespoon freshly chopped fresh tarragon
sea salt and ground black pepper

SERVES 4

An impressive dish for friends and family, the fillet/tenderloin of venison should be cooked so that it is still lovely and pink inside. (Pictured opposite.)

Heat the oven to 200°C (400°F) Gas 6.

Heat a little oil and half the butter in a frying pan/skillet and gently fry the shallots for 10 minutes until softened.

Add the garlic and mushrooms and fry for 5 minutes until the mushrooms are golden brown. Add the brandy and bubble away until reduced by half. Pour in the beef stock and cream and simmer for 5 minutes.

Season the venison. Heat an ovenproof frying pan/skillet over a high heat with a little oil. Sear the fillet all over until browned. Add the remaining butter to the frying pan/skillet and spoon over the top of the fillet.

Transfer to the oven for 5–6 minutes. Set aside to rest, loosely covered in foil.

Add the tarragon to the sauce and warm through. Serve with the venison.

FONDUE BOURGUIGNON

1.2 kg/2½ lb. potatoes, cut into cubes, plus ½ potato for the fondue pot
1.2 litres/5 cups groundnut/peanut oil or other neutral oil
4–6 sirloin steaks, cut into bite-sized strips
sea salt and ground black pepper
salad, to serve

MUSTARD SAUCE
200 ml/scant 1 cup sour cream
1–2 tablespoons Dijon mustard, to taste
a squidge of tomato ketchup

AIOLI
5–6 tablespoons mayonnaise, to taste
1 large garlic clove, crushed

FOR THE BEARNAISE SAUCE
2 tablespoons white wine vinegar
1 small shallot, finely chopped
4 black peppercorns
2 fresh tarragon stalks
2 egg yolks
200 g/¾ cup plus 2 tablespoons unsalted butter, cut into cubes
freshly squeezed lemon juice, to taste
a handful of freshly chopped tarragon
1 tablespoon extra virgin olive oil

SERVES 6

Everyone seems to know a cheese fondue, but a beef fondue, where you dip pieces of raw steak into bubbling oil, is less familiar. There is a certain flavour that the steak gets from its brief blasting in bubbling oil that is like no other. It is steak and chips like you have never eaten. The real treat is the potato hidden at the bottom of the pan, which keeps the fat from spluttering as it absorbs moisture from the meat. It can be fished out at the end, sprinkled with salt and eaten. (Pictured on pages 110-111.)

Preheat the oven to 200°C (400°F) Gas 6.

Parboil the potatoes for 5 minutes, then drain and dry in the pan over a low heat. Heat a layer of oil in a roasting pan and add the parboiled potatoes. Cook in the preheated oven for 40 minutes, turning occasionally, until golden and crisp.

Meanwhile, make the sauces. Mix the ingredients together for the mustard sauce, then the aioli, and chill them until ready to serve. For the béarnaise, put the vinegar and 1 tablespoon water in a small pan with the shallot, peppercorns and tarragon stalks. Simmer until reduced to about 2 teaspoons. Pour into

a heatproof bowl and add the egg yolks. Whisk with a good pinch of salt, then set over a pan of barely simmering water. Add the cold butter, a knob/pat at a time, whisking constantly, until you have a glossy, thick sauce. Season to taste with a little lemon juice and more salt if it needs it, and stir in the chopped tarragon. Keep warm but not hot or it will split.

Pour the oil into your fondue pot and drop in the potato half. Heat until a piece of steak cooks nicely without frazzling in 20–30 seconds, then transfer to the burner. Serve the steak to dip into the oil with the sauces, potatoes and salad.

DESSERTS

KAISERSCHMARRN

This is a mess of a pudding fit for an emperor. Although simple in its ingredients, this classic Austrian dessert tastes rich and indulgent. A deep, fluffy pancake is filled with booze-soaked raisins, shredded and dusted in icing sugar and served with a tart plum compote. Although this is really a sweet dessert dish, often in the Austrian alps this is eaten as lunch instead.

100 g/heaping ⅔ cup (dark) raisins
60 ml/¼ cup schnapps, kirsch or rum
250 g/1¾ cups plus 2 tablespoons flour
a pinch of salt
6 eggs, separated
3 tablespoons caster/superfine sugar
1 teaspoon pure vanilla extract
finely grated zest of 1 lemon
350–400 ml/1½–1¾ cups milk
50 g/3½ tablespoons butter
icing/confectioners' sugar, to dust

FOR THE PLUM COMPOTE
500 g/1lb. 2oz. plums, halved and stoned/pitted
a splash of water
50 g/¼ cup caster/superfine sugar
1 star anise
1 small cinnamon stick

30-cm/12-in. non-stick frying pan/skillet

SERVES 6–8

Make the plum compote first. Put all the ingredients into a pan and cook over a low heat for 20–30 minutes until the plums have broken down to a thick compote. Spoon into a bowl and set aside.

Put the raisins into a small pan with the schnapps and heat gently, then set aside for at least 15 minutes to allow them to plump up.

Sift the flour into a mixing bowl and add a good pinch of salt. Make a well in the centre and add the egg yolks, sugar, vanilla and lemon zest. Start stirring, adding the milk gradually, until you have a smooth batter, thicker than double/heavy cream.

Whisk the egg whites in a separate bowl until stiff peaks form, then gently fold them into the batter.

Preheat the oven to 200°C (400°F) Gas 6.

Melt the butter in the frying pan/skillet over a low heat. Pour in the batter (it will be a very thick pancake), and after a couple of minutes, when you can see it starting to set around the edge, scatter the raisins and schnapps over the top. Once the underside is set and golden brown, and it is cooked halfway through (use a small knife to cut into it), transfer to the oven for 5 minutes until golden.

Using a knife and fork, cut it into small, thin pieces – don't worry if it's still a little undercooked in the centre. Pop it back in the oven for 2–3 minutes.

Scoop onto a warmed serving plate and dust thickly with icing/confectioners' sugar. Serve immediately with the plum compote on the side.

PEAR GALETTE

200 g/1½ cups plain/all-purpose flour

a pinch of fine sea salt

125 g/½ cup plus 1 tablespoon cold unsalted butter, cut into cubes, plus 25 g/1½ tablespoons butter, melted

3 tablespoons caster/superfine sugar

1 egg yolk

1–2 tablespoons ice-cold water

3 firm but ripe pears, peeled and cored

1 tablespoon ground almonds

2 tablespoons apricot jam/jelly

baking sheet and two sheets of baking parchment

SERVES 8

A galette can mean many different things, and be both sweet and savoury. This one is based loosely on a teatime treat that I love to eat when I visit friends who live in Arbois. Their local boulangerie makes the best apple-and-pear galettes, and I can always find room for a slice. I have made this one with a sweet pastry-style base, making it easy to prepare. (Pictured on page 116.)

In a bowl, rub the flour, salt and butter cubes together with your fingertips until it resembles breadcrumbs (or pulse in a food processor). Add 2 tablespoons of the sugar, then add the egg yolk and enough ice-cold water to just bring the pastry together into a dough.

Knead briefly until smooth, then roll out between two sheets of baking parchment to a 28 cm/11 in. circle. Neaten the edge with a knife. Chill for 15–20 minutes.

Cut the pears into thin wedges. Peel the top layer of parchment off the dough (leaving it on the bottom piece) and fold and twist the edge of the circle to form a neat, crimped edge, about 1 cm/½ in. thick. Sprinkle with the ground almonds.

Preheat the oven to 200°C (400°F) Gas 6 and put in a baking sheet to heat up.

Layer the pears in circles around the inside of the tart, slightly overlapping. Brush all over with the melted butter and sprinkle with the last tablespoon of caster/superfine sugar.

Transfer the tart on its parchment to the preheated baking sheet, then bake for 25–30 minutes until the pastry is golden and the pears are tender.

Heat the apricot jam/jelly in a small pan with 1 tablespoon of water until melted. Strain into a small bowl then brush all over the top of the still warm tart. Leave to cool then serve.

MONT BLANC

2 UK large/US extra-large egg whites

a pinch of fine sea salt

120 g/⅔ cup caster/superfine sugar

150 g/5 oz. sweetened chestnut purée

75 ml/5 tablespoons double/heavy cream

2 tablespoons brandy

300 ml/generous 1¼ cups whipping cream

1 teaspoon vanilla bean paste

baking sheet, lined with baking parchment

SERVES 4

This dessert is so-named because it resembles the snowy peaks of the highest mountain in the Alps. It's a mountain of meringue topped with fluffy cream and sweetened chestnuts.

Preheat the oven to 110°C (225°F) Gas ¼. Beat the egg whites and salt in a clean bowl until they form stiff peaks. Gradually add the sugar, a little at a time, whisking constantly, until you have a thick, glossy meringue.

Scoop four peaky dollops onto the prepared baking sheet like little mountains. Bake in the oven for 2 hours, then turn the oven off and leave them to cool inside.

Whiz the chestnut purée with the double/heavy cream and brandy in a food processor or blender, until you have a smooth, spoonable sauce.

Whip the whipping cream with the vanilla bean paste until it is just holding its shape.

Place the meringues on to plates and spoon over the billowing cream. Drizzle with the chestnut sauce and serve.

PUMPKIN PANNA COTTA

200 ml/scant 1 cup whole/full-fat milk

400 ml/1¾ cups double/heavy cream

80 g/scant ½ cup caster/superfine sugar

1 teaspoon pure vanilla extract

½ teaspoon ground cinnamon

a pinch of ground cloves

4 gelatine leaves

250 g/9 oz. puréed pumpkin from a can

6 x 175-ml/¾-cup individual pudding moulds

MAKES 6

This is a truly elegant dessert, silky and smooth with a hint of spice enriching the natural sweetness of the pumpkin. Pumpkin isn't used often as a dessert ingredient in the UK, but it's popular in Europe and the US. It's such a versatile vegetable and it works brilliantly in this Italian classic.

Pour the milk and cream into a pan and add the sugar, vanilla and spices. Heat gently until the sugar dissolves, then bring just to the boil and remove from the heat.

Soak the gelatine in a bowl of cold water for a couple of minutes until soft, then squeeze out as much water as possible. Add to the hot cream mixture and stir until dissolved.

Add the pumpkin purée and pour into a jug/pitcher.

Rinse the pudding moulds with cold water then pour the panna cotta mixture into them. Put them on a tray and chill for at least 3 hours.

To serve, dip each mould briefly into hot water, then invert onto a plate. Serve with whipped sweetened cream.

CRÊPES

125 g/1 cup minus 1 tablespoon plain/all-purpose flour

1 teaspoon caster/superfine sugar

a pinch of fine sea salt

1 egg, lightly beaten

300 ml/generous 1¼ cups whole/full-fat milk

vegetable oil, to grease

TOPPING IDEAS

sliced banana and chocolate spread

lemon and sugar

maple syrup

apple compote and Chantilly cream

25-cm/10-in. non-stick frying pan/skillet

SERVES 8

A French pancake or crêpe is lacy thin, and, to confuse matters, it can also sometimes be called a galette when it is made with buckwheat flour. Crêpes can be filled with whatever you fancy, and they are also delicious as a savoury dish filled with melting cheese and ham. If you are going to make them savoury, omit the teaspoon of sugar from the mixture.

Sift the flour into a bowl and add the sugar and salt. Make a well in the centre and add the egg. Start to stir with a wooden spoon, slowly incorporating the flour into the mixture.

Gradually add the milk, stirring all the time, drawing in the flour until you have a smooth, thin batter. Set aside to rest for 10 minutes.

Pour a tiny amount of oil into the frying pan/skillet and wipe it out with a paper towel. Place over a medium–high heat.

Pour in a small ladleful of the batter and swirl around the pan to coat. You can pour out any excess batter as you make them – you will get better at judging the amount of batter you need. It should thinly coat the bottom of the pan.

Cook for 30 seconds then flip the crêpe over and cook for a further 30–45 seconds. Slide onto a warmed plate and keep warm as you cook the rest of the crêpes. Top with your choice of ingredients and devour.

APFELSTRUDEL

True strudel pastry is a work of art and well worth the effort of making your own. If you want to, you can use well-buttered layers of filo pastry instead, but it just doesn't have quite the same texture, because it becomes quite brittle when baked. The art of strudel dough-making is getting it as thin as possible. You want to be able to read a newspaper through your dough when you have finished.

350 g/2⅔ cups plain/all-purpose flour

3 tablespoons neutral oil, such as vegetable oil, plus extra to grease

150–200 ml/scant ⅔–scant 1 cup lukewarm water

a pinch of fine sea salt

melted butter, to brush

2–3 tablespoons ground almonds

500 g/1 lb. 2 oz. cooking apples, peeled and chopped

a handful of sultanas/golden raisins

150 g/¾ cup plus 1 tablespoon caster/superfine sugar, plus extra to sprinkle

1 teaspoon ground cinnamon

a squeeze of lemon juice

SERVES 6–8

Mix the flour, oil and water together with a good pinch of salt to form a soft dough. Knead the dough for 5 minutes until smooth and elastic, then pop into a lightly oiled bowl and leave to stand in a warm place, covered with a layer of clingfilm/plastic wrap, for about 1 hour to rest. It might seem unusual to rest pastry in a warm place, but it will help you to be able to stretch it out later.

Roll the dough with a rolling pin on a board to a rectangle about 25 × 30cm/10 × 12 in. Cover your table with a clean, smooth cloth, then flip the strudel dough onto the centre of the cloth.

You now need to stretch the dough carefully with your hands. Think of it as a large pizza. Reach under the dough to the centre and, very gently, using the back of your hand (using your fingertips is more likely to cause tears), stretch the dough. Try to keep it in as much of a rectangle as possible. You want to end up with a very large rectangle, about 75 × 50 cm/30 × 20 in. in size.

Try to make the dough as even as possible. If you do make any little tears, pinch the dough together to patch them up. Once you have a very thin, large rectangle – so thin you could read through it – trim or snip off the edges.

Preheat the oven to 220°C (425°F) Gas 7.

Brush the dough all over with melted butter and sprinkle with ground almonds. Mix the apples, sultanas/golden raisins, sugar and cinnamon together with a squeeze of lemon juice. Pile this filling along the bottom half of the dough, about 20 cm/8 in. from the bottom, leaving about 6 cm/2½ in. on each side.

Using the cloth to help you, flip the bottom of the dough over to cover the filling. Tuck the edges in to make them neat. Then, as you would roll a Swiss/jelly roll, use the cloth to roll up the strudel. Roll it onto a sheet of baking parchment and place on a baking sheet.

Brush all over with more melted butter and sprinkle with a little sugar. Bake for 20 minutes, then reduce the oven to 190°C (375°F) Gas 5 and bake for a further 20 minutes until golden. Cool a little, then serve, sliced, with cream.

GERMKNÖDEL

500 g/3½ cups strong white bread flour

1 teaspoon fine sea salt

3 tablespoons caster/superfine sugar

30 g/1 oz. fresh yeast (or 2 × 7-g/¼-oz. sachets dried yeast)

250 ml/generous 1 cup whole/full-fat milk, warmed

35 g/2 tablespoons plus 1 teaspoon butter, melted and cooled, plus extra melted butter, to brush

2 eggs, beaten

10 generous teaspoons plum jam/jelly

poppy seeds, to serve

FOR THE VANILLA SAUCE

500 ml/2 cups whole/full-fat milk

2 tablespoons cornflour/cornstarch

2 egg yolks

200 g/1 cup plus 2 tablespoons caster/superfine sugar

2 tablespoons vanilla extract

60 g/¼ cup butter, melted

baking sheet, lightly greased

SERVES 10

The germknödel is a cross between a doughnut and a steamed bun. This recipe was something of a revelation to me. I had never eaten a germknödel on my skiing travels – a dish that so many people had told me was such a wonderful treat – and so I wondered what was in store. With excitement and trepidation, I lifted the lid on my steamer to reveal beautifully plump, sweet-and-tender dough buns filled with sharp plum jam. These are honestly one of the most delicious things I have ever tasted.

Mix the flour with the salt and sugar in a large bowl. Mix the yeast with a couple of tablespoons of the warm milk and leave to stand for a few minutes until it starts to froth. Add this, along with the rest of the milk, the melted butter and the eggs, to the flour. Mix to form a soft dough.

Turn out onto a lightly floured surface and knead vigorously for 10 minutes. Put back in the bowl (give it a quick wash first) and cover with a clean dishtowel. Leave to rise somewhere warm for 1 hour or so until it has doubled in size.

Knock back/punch down your dough, then divide into 10 pieces. Flatten each piece out on the work surface then dollop a spoonful of the jam/jelly into the centre. Bring the dough around the jam/jelly and seal well by pinching the edges together with your fingers.

Place on the prepared baking sheet and cover with the dishtowel. Leave for 30 minutes–1 hour until doubled in size.

Make the sauce. Heat the milk in a pan until almost boiling. Whisk the cornflour/cornstarch, egg yolks, sugar and vanilla together in a bowl, then pour over the hot milk. Return to the pan and put over a low heat. Cook, stirring, until thick. Add the melted butter and keep warm while you steam the buns.

Bring a very large pan of water to the boil – you can use a bamboo steamer or a normal steamer lined with baking parchment, otherwise you can use the traditional Austrian method: brush a clean cotton dish towel with melted butter and put over the pan, then secure in place with twine, making sure no cloth is exposed to the heat source. Put the dumplings, a few at a time, on top of the steamer. Cover with the steamer lid or a second large pan. Steam for 15 minutes.

Brush with a little melted butter and scatter with poppy seeds. Serve the dumplings with the vanilla sauce to smother over the top.

2 eggs

300 ml/generous 1¼ cups whole/full-fat milk

250 g/1¾ cups plus 2 tablespoons plain/all-purpose flour

2 teaspoons baking powder

a good pinch of fine sea salt

1 tablespoon caster/superfine sugar

75 g/⅓ cup unsalted butter, melted and cooled

maple syrup, to serve

FOR THE FRUIT

300 g/2⅓ cups frozen forest fruits

75 g/⅓ cup plus 1 tablespoon caster/superfine sugar

1 vanilla pod/bean, halved and seeds scraped

FOR THE CHANTILLY CREAM

200 ml/scant 1 cup whipping cream

2 tablespoons icing/confectioners' sugar

waffle iron

SERVES 8

GAUFRES

Although waffles are often eaten as a breakfast in the US, I love a waffle as a dessert. This recipe uses a waffle iron, which is really easy to buy, but if you don't have one you could make these on a wide ridged griddle pan instead.

Whisk the eggs and milk together in a bowl, then sprinkle in the flour, baking powder, salt and sugar. Whisk together until just incorporated. Pour in the cooled melted butter and whisk until it is just combined. Don't overmix or your waffles will be tough. Set aside while you make the fruit and cream.

Put the fruit, sugar and vanilla seeds into a pan and bubble until you have a rich, glossy fruit purée.

Whip the cream and icing/confectioners' sugar together until light and fluffy

Preheat the waffle iron and lightly grease it, then cook 4–5 tablespoons of the batter at a time (depending on your waffle iron) into golden, fluffy waffles.

Serve the warm waffles drizzled with maple syrup, and accompanied by the fruit and Chantilly cream on the side.

CLASSIC TARTE TATIN

200 g/1 cup plus 2 tablespoons caster/superfine sugar

50 g/3½ tablespoons cold unsalted butter, cut into cubes

4 fresh thyme sprigs

8–9 dessert apples such as Braeburn, peeled, cored and halved

plain/all-purpose flour, to dust

375 g/13 oz. block all-butter puff pastry

20-cm/8-in. ovenproof frying pan/skillet

SERVES 6–8

A tarte tatin, with its crisp golden pastry, sticky caramel and tender, sweet and sharp apples, has to be one of the best desserts going. It can be prepared in advance, ready to just pop into the oven to cook before serving. (Opposite.)

Put the sugar in the frying pan/skillet with 2 tablespoons water and put over a low heat. Do not stir. Once the sugar has completely dissolved, increase the heat and bubble until you have a rich mahogany-brown caramel.

Remove from the heat and add the butter, it will bubble and foam. Put the thyme and apples into the caramel, cut-side up, packing them close together as they will shrink a bit in cooking. Place back over a low heat and cook for 5 minutes or so, then remove them from the heat and cool completely.

Preheat the oven to 200°C (400°F) Gas 6.

On a lightly floured surface, roll out the pastry until it is 3 mm/⅛ in. thick. Cut out a rough 25 cm/10 in. disc of pastry and tuck it over the apples. Tuck the edges of the pastry around the sides of the apples.

Bake in the oven for 30 minutes until the pastry is golden and puffed up. Leave to stand for 5 minutes then invert the tart onto a serving plate. Serve with vanilla ice cream.

TARTE AUX MYRTILLES

175 g/1⅓ cups plain/all-purpose flour

100 g/½ cup minus 1 tablespoon cold unsalted butter, cut into cubes

3 tablespoons icing/confectioners' sugar

1–2 tablespoons milk

350 g/2¾ cups bilberries or blueberries (or a mix of blueberries and blackcurrants)

3 tablespoons sour cream

3 tablespoons caster/superfine sugar

2 eggs, beaten

23-cm/9-in. shallow tart pan

SERVES 6

Although the word myrtille is translated as a blueberry, the mountain blueberry found in Europe is actually a bilberry: a relation of the blueberry but smaller and much sharper in its flavour, a bit like a cross between a blueberry and a blackcurrant. Blueberries are an excellent substitute.

Preheat the oven to 200°C (400°F) Gas 6.

Put the flour in a bowl and add the butter and icing/confectioners' sugar, then rub together with your fingers until it resembles breadcrumbs. Add the milk and mix until you have a dough. Knead briefly then chill for 10 minutes.

Roll out on a lightly floured surface and use to line the tart pan. Chill for another 10 minutes or so.

Line the pastry with baking parchment and baking beans or rice and bake in the preheated oven for 12–15 minutes

then remove the paper and beans and return for a further couple of minutes until lightly golden and crisp. Turn the oven down to 180°C (350°F) Gas 4.

Tip the berries into the tart in a single layer and return to the oven for 15 minutes. Mix the sour cream, caster/superfine sugar and eggs together then pour over the berries.

Cook for a further 15 minutes. Turn the oven off and leave to cool in the oven for 15–20 minutes, then serve warm with lots of cream or sour cream.

BUTTER TARTS

250 g/1¾ cups plus 2 tablespoons plain/all-purpose flour, plus extra to dust

2 tablespoons caster/superfine sugar

a good pinch of fine sea salt

100 g/½ cup minus 1 tablespoon cold unsalted butter, cut into cubes

75 g/⅓ cup cold lard, cut into cubes

1 egg yolk

2–3 tablespoons ice-cold water

FOR THE FILLING

2 eggs

100 g/½ cup light muscovado sugar

75 ml/5 tablespoons maple syrup

1 teaspoon pure vanilla extract

100 ml/scant ½ cup double/heavy cream

60 g/¼ cup unsalted butter

50 g/½ cup chopped walnuts or pecan nuts

125 g/scant 1 cup (dark) raisins

2 x 12-hole tart pans

MAKES 24

A wonderful Canadian speciality, these tarts are a little like a treacle tart but without the breadcrumbs. Everyone I asked had their own recipe, but this is my version, simple and sweet with a rich hint of maple syrup and a hit of nuts. I like these warm with a drizzle of cream. (Pictured opposite.)

Mix the flour with the sugar and salt. Either in a food processor or with your fingertips, rub in the cold butter and lard until it resembles breadcrumbs. Add the egg yolk and then add enough cold water to bring the mixture together. Knead briefly into a smooth dough then shape into a disc and chill for 10 minutes.

Roll out on a lightly floured surface and cut out 24 discs 7.5 cm/3 in. in diameter using a fluted cutter. Line the tart pans with the pastry and chill in the fridge while you make the filling.

Preheat the oven to 190°C (375°F) Gas 5.

Beat the eggs with the sugar, syrup, vanilla and cream. Pour into a pan, add the butter and cook over a low heat until the butter is melted and the mixture thickens and coats the back of the spoon. Remove from the heat. Stir in the nuts and raisins. Divide between the tart shells.

Bake for 16–18 minutes until the filling is set and golden. Cool for a few minutes before turning out. Serve warm or cold.

HUCKLEBERRY PIE

300 g/2¼ cups plain/all-purpose flour, plus extra to dust

2 teaspoons caster/superfine sugar

a good pinch of fine sea salt

150 g/⅔ cup cold unsalted butter, cut into cubes

60 g/¼ cup cold lard, cut into pieces

1 teaspoon cider vinegar

3 tablespoons cold water

caster/superfine sugar, to sprinkle

FOR THE FILLING

350 g/2¾ cups huckleberries or blueberries

75 g/⅓ cup plus 1 tablespoon caster/superfine sugar, plus extra to sprinkle

finely grated zest of 1 orange and 1 lemon

a good squeeze of lemon juice

4 tablespoons cornflour/cornstarch

1 egg, beaten

23-cm/9-in. pie dish

SERVES 8

The Alps have their myrtle berries and bilberries, and the American mountains have their huckleberries, another smaller, tarter relation to the blueberry. Huckleberry pie is as famous a US dessert as you can get.

Mix the flour with the sugar and salt. Either in a food processor or with your fingertips, rub in the cold butter and lard until it resembles breadcrumbs. Add the vinegar and enough cold water to bring the mixture together. Knead briefly into a smooth dough then shape into two discs, one a little larger than the other. Chill in the fridge for 10 minutes.

Roll out the bigger half of dough on a lightly floured surface to 3 mm/⅛ in. thick and use to line the base of the pie dish. Trim so that it comes up about 1 cm/½ in. over the edge and add any leftover pastry to the other half of dough. Chill while you make the filling.

Preheat the oven to 190°C (375°F) Gas 5.

Put one-quarter of the berries with the sugar, citrus zest and juice in a pan, and cook over a low heat until the berries begin to burst. Allow to cool, then mix with the cornflour/cornstarch and the rest of the berries. Tip into the pie dish.

Roll out the remaining pastry to 3 mm/⅛ in. thick and put on the pie. Crimp the edges together. Cut a couple of slits in the top and brush all over with beaten egg. Sprinkle with a little extra sugar and bake for 35–40 minutes until golden and crisp. Cool then serve with slightly sweetened cream.

PRUNE AND ARMAGNAC SOUFFLÉ

200 g/scant 2 cups pitted prunes

50 ml/scant ¼ cup Armagnac

1 teaspoon pure vanilla extract

1 teaspoon fennel seeds, wrapped in a small piece of muslin and tied into a bag

20 g/2⅓ tablespoons plain/all-purpose flour

20 g/1½ tablespoons butter, plus melted butter, to brush

75 g/⅓ cup plus 1 tablespoon caster/superfine sugar, plus extra for dusting

200 ml/scant 1 cup whole/full-fat milk

2 egg yolks and 3 egg whites

6 small scoops vanilla ice cream

6 x 175-ml/¾-cup ramekins

SERVES 6

A soufflé is a thing of great beauty. You delve into its depths to find the soft, almost gooey centre and, in this case, a hit of sweet prunes and Armagnac. Don't fear the soufflé, they are actually far more robust than a lot of people make out. You can even take them from the oven, dig in a spoon to see if it has reached perfect cookedness and pop it back in the oven if it isn't ready, and they will be none the worse for wear.

Put the prunes in a small pan with the Armagnac, vanilla and fennel, and heat gently until steaming. Remove from the heat and leave to stand overnight. Discard the fennel seeds in the bag then remove 6 prunes. Purée the remaining prunes with the juices in a food processor or blender until really smooth. Set aside.

Put the flour, butter and 2 tablespoons of the caster/superfine sugar in a bowl and rub together with your fingertips to resemble breadcrumbs. Bring the milk to just below the boil then whisk in the flour and butter mixture. Cook, stirring constantly, over a low heat until you have a thick sauce. Remove from the heat and beat in the 2 egg yolks. Spoon into a bowl and set aside to cool completely, place a layer of clingfilm/plastic wrap on the surface to stop a skin forming.

Brush the ramekins with melted butter, then dust the insides with sugar. Put on a baking sheet. Preheat the oven to 200°C (400°F) Gas 6.

Once cooled, fold the prune purée through the custard mixture. Whisk the egg whites to stiff peaks, then gradually whisk in the remaining caster sugar until you have a glossy meringue mixture. Mix a spoonful of this into the prune custard to loosen it, then carefully fold in the rest. Spoon into the ramekins so they are just over three-quarters full. Bake for 12–15 minutes until risen and firm with a slight wobble.

Cut a slit in the top of each, push in a soaked prune and top with a scoop of the ice cream. Serve immediately.

BAKED APPLES WITH CALVADOS

60 g/½ cup sultanas/golden raisins

3 tablespoons calvados

25 g/2 tablespoons caster/superfine sugar

25 g/1 tablespoon plus 2 teaspoons soft brown sugar

50 g/3½ tablespoons unsalted butter, softened

4 firm apples, such as Braeburn or russet, cored

FOR THE SAUCE

50 g/¼ cup caster/superfine sugar

50 ml/scant ¼ cup apple juice

2 tablespoons calvados

25 g/1 tablespoon plus 2 teaspoons unsalted butter

double/heavy cream or vanilla ice cream and toasted flaked almonds, to serve

SERVES 4

A baked apple is a wonder. The texture that you get from baking an apple whole in its skin, allowing the flesh to steam and soften, is like no other. Here the apple is cooked with some of its closest friends – butter, sugar, dried fruit and apple brandy – to make a pudding that is unsurpassed in its ability to comfort and soothe. (Pictured on page 133.)

Preheat the oven to 180°C (350°F) Gas 4.

Put the sultanas/golden raisins in a small pan with the calvados and bring to the boil, then remove from the heat and allow to cool in the calvados. Mix the sugars with the butter and add the soaked cooled sultanas.

Put the apples in a small roasting pan. Stuff the apples with the filling and bake in the oven for 30 minutes until the apples are just tender.

Meanwhile, make the sauce. Put the sugar in a pan with 1 tablespoon of water and dissolve over a low heat, without stirring. Once it's melted, turn up the heat and boil until you have a dark caramel. Remove from the heat and add the apple juice, calvados and butter. Stir until smooth.

Serve the sauce over the apples with lots of cream or ice cream and a sprinkling of toasted flaked almonds.

CRÈME BRÛLÉE

600 ml/generous 2½ cups double/heavy cream

1 vanilla pod/bean

6 egg yolks

4 tablespoons caster/superfine sugar, plus extra to sprinkle

6 x 200-ml/1-cup ramekins

SERVES 6

Under the satisfying crack of the caramel lid lies the smoothest of smooth custards, set to perfection. It is worth investing in a little cook's blowtorch for these as it makes caramelizing the top such a doddle. (Pictured opposite.)

Preheat the oven to 150°C (300°F) Gas 2. Put the ramekins in a roasting pan.

Pour the cream into a pan. Halve the vanilla pod/bean and scrape out the seeds, then add both to the pan. Cook over a medium heat until just about boiling. Remove from the heat.

In a bowl, whisk the egg yolks with the caster/superfine sugar, then gradually pour over the hot cream and whisk until combined. Strain into a jug/pitcher.

Divide the custard between the ramekins and slide into the oven. Pour boiling water around the ramekins until it comes about halfway up the sides. Bake in the preheated oven for 35–40 minutes until just set, then remove from the oven.

Take the ramekins out of the pan and let cool, then chill until cold.

Scatter the top of each custard with a teaspoon of sugar. Use a blowtorch to caramelize the top of the custards. If you don't have one, preheat the grill/broiler to high and pop the custards under the grill/broiler to caramelize. Pop back in the fridge until cold again. Serve with little buttery biscuits.

CAKES, PASTRIES AND BAKING

ESTERHAZY CAKE

FOR THE SPONGE

400 g/3 cups blanched hazelnuts

3 tablespoons plain/all-purpose flour

9 egg whites

200 g/1 cup plus 2 tablespoons caster/superfine sugar

FOR THE FILLING

9 egg yolks

200 g/1 cup plus 2 tablespoons caster/superfine sugar

1 teaspoon pure vanilla extract

225 g/1 cup unsalted butter, softened

20 g/scant ¼ cup unsweetened cocoa powder

FOR THE TOP

3 tablespoons apricot jam/jelly

40 g/1½ oz. dark/bittersweet chocolate

3 teaspoons vegetable oil

300 g/2 cups plus 2 tablespoons icing/confectioners' sugar

1 tablespoon freshly squeezed lemon juice

warm water

2 baking sheets, lined with baking parchment

small disposable piping/pastry bag

SERVES 12–14

This beautiful hazelnut layer cake is a labour of love, but it's worth every second. I love the way the cake looks, with its spider's web icing. Once I got over my initial shock at how many layers this cake needed, I found it to be a simple cake masquerading as a technical challenge.

Preheat the oven to 160°C (325°F) Gas 3.

Put the hazelnuts on a baking sheet and roast for 20 minutes. Cool and then blitz in a food processor until roughly chopped. Take out 150 g/scant 1¼ cups and set aside. Add the flour to the food processor and blitz to fine crumbs.

In a clean bowl, whisk the egg whites to stiff peaks, then whisk in the sugar, a spoonful at a time, until you have a smooth, glossy meringue. Fold in the hazelnut and flour mixture. Take the lined baking sheets and draw on five 20 cm/8 in. circles. Divide the mixture among the circles and spread evenly. Bake for 16 minutes until golden brown and not sticky to the touch. You may need to do this in batches.

Make the filling. Put the egg yolks, sugar and vanilla in a heatproof bowl and set over a pan of barely simmering water. Whisk with an electric hand whisk until pale and voluminous. Remove from the water and whisk for a few more minutes then let cool completely. Beat the butter until light and fluffy, then fold in the cooled egg mixture and cocoa powder.

Peel all the meringues off the baking parchment. Put one on a clean piece of baking parchment on a baking sheet and spread with about one-quarter of the filling. Top with another meringue and layer up in this fashion, ending with a meringue, but reserving a little buttercream. Use the remaining buttercream to spread around the outside of the cake. Top with another

piece of parchment then put a baking sheet on top. Weigh down with a couple of cans and chill for 1 hour.

Melt the apricot jam/jelly in a pan with 1 tablespoon water, then push it through a sieve/strainer until smooth. Put the chilled cake on a cake plate, still on its bottom layer of parchment. Spread the apricot jam over the top. Chill for 10 minutes.

Melt the chocolate with half the oil in a small heatproof bowl set over a pan of barely simmering water. Pour into the piping/pastry bag and set aside.

Whisk the icing/confectioners' sugar and lemon with the remaining oil, then gradually add warm water, a little at a time, until you have a smooth, spreadable glaze. Pour about half the glaze over the cake and smooth it out – don't worry if it drips down the side. You can add more glaze if you need to – you want to create a really smooth layer. Snip a small hole at the bottom of the chocolate piping bag and pipe a spiral of chocolate over the icing. Use the tip of a sharp knife to drag six lines from the centre of the cake to the outside. In between each outward line, drag the tip of the knife back into the centre of the cake to create a spider's web effect.

Clean the sides of the cake with a spatula and press the reserved chopped hazelnuts around the edge. Chill the cake overnight.

Carefully remove the parchment from the base and pop the cake back on your cake plate and you are ready to serve.

CARROT CAKE

4 eggs

225 ml/¾ cup plus 3 tablespoons sunflower oil

100 g/½ cup plus 1 tablespoon caster/superfine sugar

100 g/½ cup soft light brown sugar

300 g/2¼ cups self-raising/self-rising flour

a good pinch of ground cinnamon

1 teaspoon baking powder

½ teaspoon bicarbonate of soda/baking soda

4 large carrots (about 350 g/12 oz.), grated

60 g/½ cup pine nuts, toasted

a little milk, if needed

FOR THE ICING

600 g/2⅔ cups cream cheese

300 ml/1¼ cups double/heavy cream

2 teaspoons pure vanilla extract

125 g/heaping ¾ cup icing/confectioners' sugar, plus extra to taste (optional)

20-cm/8-in. loose-bottomed cake pan, greased and lined

SERVES 10

Even though I have always known that the use of vegetables in baking dates back to Medieval times when sugar was scarce, I had always believed that carrot cake was an American cake that had been adopted in Europe. On my research into the history of the carrot cake, however, I found that it actually originated from Europe, particularly Switzerland and Austria. Wherever it hails from, a really good carrot cake is top of most teatime lists.

Preheat the oven to 180°C (350°F) Gas 4.

Put the eggs, oil and sugars in a bowl and whisk with an electric hand whisk until the mixture is pale and creamy.

Fold through the remaining ingredients. If the batter is a little thick, add a splash of milk to loosen it.

Pour into the prepared cake pan and bake on the centre shelf of the preheated oven for 1–1¼ hours or until a skewer pushed into the centre of the cake comes out clean.

Let cool in the pan for 10 minutes. Turn out onto a wire rack to cool completely.

To make the icing, beat the cream cheese with the cream, vanilla extract and icing/confectioners' sugar until the mixture is smooth and creamy. Add more icing/confectioners' sugar to taste, if you like it a bit sweeter.

Once the cake is cool, slice it in half horizontally and spread one half with icing. Top with the other half of cake then cover with the rest of the icing.

BANANA CAKE

150 g/⅔ cup unsalted butter

150 g/¾ cup light muscovado sugar

4 tablespoons maple syrup

2 UK large/US extra-large eggs, lightly beaten

200 g/1½ cups plain/all-purpose flour, plus extra for dusting

100 g/¾ cup wholemeal/wholewheat flour

1 teaspoon bicarbonate of soda/baking soda

3 very ripe bananas, mashed

150 ml/scant ⅔ cup natural/plain yogurt

50 g/⅓ cup plain/semisweet chocolate chips

50 g/½ cup pecan nuts, chopped

2-litre/8-cup loaf pan, greased and lined

SERVES 8

I spend my life buying bunches of bananas, eating a couple and then leaving the rest to sit in the fruit bowl, looking at me as they turn from yellow to a mottled brown. This is the moment to make a loaf of sweet-smelling banana bread.

Preheat the oven to 180°C (350°F) Gas 4.

Beat the butter with the sugar and maple syrup until fluffy, then add the eggs, flours and bicarbonate of soda/baking soda.

Mash the bananas with a fork, then fold into the mixture with the yogurt chocolate and pecans. Spoon into the prepared loaf pan and level the top.

Bake in the preheated oven for 1 hour–1 hour 10 minutes until a skewer inserted in the centre comes out clean. Cover the top with foil if it starts to brown too quickly.

Allow to cool in the pan for at least 15 minutes before turning out onto a wire rack to cool completely.

ORANGE CAKE WITH RUM DRIZZLE

1 large orange
1 lemon
100 ml/scant ½ cup extra virgin olive oil
180 g/1 cup caster/superfine sugar
4 eggs
25 g/3 tablespoons plain/all-purpose flour
150 g/1½ cups ground almonds
2 teaspoons baking powder

FOR THE DRIZZLE
10 tablespoons caster/superfine sugar
freshly squeezed juice of 2 oranges
3 cloves
120 ml/scant ½ cup rum

*20-cm/8-in. loose-bottomed cake pan,
greased and lined*

SERVES 6

One of the most important rituals of skiing holidays is tea and cake when you come in off the pistes, cheeks glowing and feeling deserving of a treat. This cake reminds me of that: something sweet and sticky to eat with a warming cup of tea.

Put the whole orange and lemon in a pan and cover with water. Bring to the boil and simmer for 30 minutes until soft. Drain and allow to cool.

Halve the cooked fruit and remove the pips, then whiz them in a food processor until they form a purée.

Preheat the oven to 180°C (350°F) Gas 4.

Beat the oil, sugar and eggs together until light and fluffy. Fold in the flour, almonds and baking powder, then add the puréed fruit. Pour into the prepared cake pan.

Bake for 45–50 minutes until golden and risen, and a skewer inserted into the centre comes out clean.

Meanwhile, make the drizzle. Melt the sugar with the orange juice in a small pan, then add the cloves, bring to the boil and bubble until it becomes syrupy. Add the rum.

Pierce the cake all over with a skewer and pour over half the drizzle while the cake is still warm.

Allow to cool then serve with the rest of the drizzle.

ZUGER KIRSCHTORTE

FOR THE MERINGUE
20 g/3 tablespoons plus 1 teaspoon cornflour/cornstarch
100 g/1 cup ground almonds
4 egg whites
150 g/¾ cup plus 1 tablespoon caster/superfine sugar

FOR THE CAKE
3 eggs, separated
85g/⅓ cup plus 2 tablespoons caster/superfine sugar
50 g/6 tablespoons plain/all-purpose flour
50 g/½ cup cornflour/cornstarch
½ teaspoon baking powder

FOR THE BUTTERCREAM
150 g/⅔ cup unsalted butter, softened
100 g/scant ¾ cup icing/confectioners' sugar
3 tablespoons blackcurrant jam/jelly

FOR THE KIRSCH SYRUP
25 g/2 tablespoons caster/superfine sugar
2 tablespoons water
120 ml/scant ½ cup kirsch

FOR THE DECORATION
100 g/1¼ cups toasted flaked/slivered almonds
icing/confectioners' sugar, to dust

2 baking sheets, lined with baking parchment

23-cm/9-in. loose-bottomed cake pan, greased and lined

SERVES 8

The Swiss love, really love, their pastries, perhaps even more than the French or any other country in Europe. Teatime is treated very seriously, and with it comes cake – beautiful, delicate layers and layers of cake. Zuger kirschtorte is not just any cake, but fine Genoese sponges, meringues and buttercream, all assembled and decorated into an edible work of art.

Preheat the oven to 160°C (325°F) Gas 3. Take the lined baking sheets and draw a 23 cm/9 in. circle on each.

Make the meringues first (you can do this a day in advance, if you like). Whiz the cornflour/cornstarch and almonds together in a food processor. Beat the egg whites until they form stiff peaks. Whisk in the sugar, a little at a time, until you have a smooth, glossy meringue. Fold in the almond mixture.

Divide the mixture between the two circles and spread evenly. Bake in the preheated oven for 40–45 minutes until lightly golden. Turn off the oven and allow the meringues to cool. Remove from the oven once cool and set aside.

For the cake, preheat the oven to 170°C (340°F) Gas 3½.

Beat the egg yolks and caster/superfine sugar in a heatproof bowl set over a pan of barely simmering water with an electric hand whisk until light and fluffy. Sift over the flour, cornflour/cornstarch and baking powder, and carefully fold in.

Whisk the egg whites in a clean bowl until they form stiff peaks. Fold the egg whites into the egg yolk mixture until just incorporated.

Spoon into the prepared cake pan and bake in the preheated oven for 20–25 minutes until golden and a skewer inserted into the centre comes away clean. Turn out onto a wire rack to cool completely.

Meanwhile, make the buttercream and kirsch syrup. For the buttercream, beat the butter and icing/confectioners' sugar together until light and fluffy, then beat in the jam/jelly. Set aside.

For the kirsch syrup, put the sugar and water in a small pan and cook over a low heat until the sugar is melted. Add the kirsch and leave to cool.

Assemble the cake. Carefully peel the meringues off the baking parchment. Put one on a cake plate and spread one-third of the buttercream over the top. Put the cake on top, then spoon over the kirsch syrup. Spread one-third more of the buttercream over the cake and top with the other meringue.

Use the last of the buttercream to coat the outside of the cake, then press the almonds around the outside.

Dust with icing/confectioners' sugar, then use the back of a knife to make a criss-cross pattern.

GATEAU DE SAVOIE

6 UK large/US extra-large eggs, separated

1 teaspoon pure vanilla extract

200 g/1½ cups minus 1 tablespoon icing/confectioners' sugar, plus extra to dust

60 ml/¼ cup boiling water

¼ teaspoon cream of tartar

175 g/1⅓ cups plain/all-purpose flour

100 g/¾ cup chopped mixed/candied peel

finely grated zest of 1 lemon

icing/confectioners' sugar, to dust

TO SERVE

a jar of cherries in kirsch

whipped cream

25-cm/10-in. bundt pan, greased with butter and dusted with icing/confectioners' sugar

SERVES 10–12

Though simple, this classic Alpine cake from the Savoie is one of the true delights I came across when writing this book. It is feather light with a hint of citrus and a lovely crust that begs to be smothered in cream and cherries. This would make an excellent dessert as well as an indulgent teatime treat.

Preheat the oven to 150°C (300°F) Gas 2.

Whisk the egg yolks, vanilla extract and icing/confectioners' sugar in the bowl of a stand mixer or with an electric hand whisk, until very thick, creamy and beautifully pale. As you whisk, very slowly dribble in the boiling water, a tiny bit at a time. Once all the water is added, keep whisking until you have a thick, glossy mixture that holds its shape.

In a clean bowl, whisk the egg whites with the cream of tartar until they form stiff peaks.

Sift the flour over the egg yolk mixture, folding in as you go. Fold in the peel and lemon zest. Mix a large dollop of the egg white into the mixture to loosen it a little, then carefully fold in the rest, trying not to knock out too much air.

Scrape into the pan and bake in the preheated oven for 50 minutes–1 hour until golden and a skewer pushed into the centre comes away clean. Turn out onto a wire rack to cool completely.

Dust with icing/confectioners' sugar and serve with the kirsch-soaked cherries and lots of cream.

PUNSCHKRAPFEN

4 eggs, separated

1½ tablespoons warm water

150 g/¾ cup plus 1 tablespoon caster/superfine sugar

1 teaspoon pure vanilla extract

150 g/1½ cups ground almonds

50 g/½ cup cornflour/cornstarch

FOR THE FILLING

150 g/½ cup apricot jam/jelly

100 g/3¾ oz. nougat

30 g/3½ tablespoons icing/confectioners' sugar

20 g/scant ¼ cup unsweetened cocoa powder

2 tablespoons freshly squeezed lemon juice

2 teaspoons rum

FOR THE ICING

200 g/scant 1½ cups icing/confectioners' sugar

a squeeze of lemon juice

1–2 tablespoons water

pink food colouring

1 tablespoon rum

23 x 30-cm/9 x 12-in. brownie pan, greased and lined

4-cm/1½-in. square cake cutter

MAKES 10

A little bit like a very grown up fondant fancy, these little cakey treats look as pretty as a picture and are almost tooth-achingly sweet. Traditionally, they are pink but I quite like the idea of them being a rainbow of colours.

Preheat the oven to 200°C (400°F) Gas 6.

Beat the egg yolks with the warm water, sugar and vanilla until very light and fluffy. Fold in the ground almonds and cornflour/cornstarch. Whisk the egg whites in a clean bowl until holding stiff peaks, then gently fold into the egg yolk mixture. Pour into the prepared cake pan and spread evenly.

Bake in the oven for 10–12 minutes until golden and a skewer inserted into the centre comes out clean. Turn out onto a wire rack to cool completely.

Cut out 20 squares from the cake using the 4-cm/1½-in. square cutter. Crumble the rest of the cake (you need about 200 g/7 oz.) into a bowl.

Melt the apricot jam/jelly with the nougat, icing/confectioners' sugar, cocoa and lemon juice in a pan, then stir in the cake crumbs and rum.

Take the cutter and put a piece of cake at the bottom, fill with the cake crumb mixture, then top with a second square of cake. Leave to cool. Repeat with the remaining cakes and cake crumb mixture to make 10 punschkrapfen.

For the icing, mix the icing/confectioners' sugar with the lemon juice, food colouring, rum and 1–2 tablespoons water to achieve a pouring consistency similar to golden/light corn syrup.

Carefully dip each cake into the icing, then put on a wire rack to dry.

MADELEINES

4 eggs

200 g/1 cup plus 2 tablespoons caster/superfine sugar, plus 2 tablespoons extra

200 g/1½ cups plain/all-purpose flour

1½ teaspoons baking powder

2 teaspoons pure vanilla extract

200 g/¾ cup plus 2 tablespoons unsalted butter, melted and cooled

pearled or nibbed sugar, to sprinkle (optional)

12-hole madeleine mould, lightly brushed with melted butter and lightly dusted with flour, any excess flour tipped out

MAKES 24

These are pretty little shell-like cakes that you can pop into your mouth and devour in just a couple of small bites. They are baked in a scallop-shaped tray to give them their distinctive shape. Try them too with little chocolate chunks or dried fruit and candied peel.

Whisk the eggs and sugar together until light and fluffy then whisk in the flour, baking powder, vanilla and melted cooled butter. Leave the mixture to stand for 20 minutes.

Preheat the oven to 200°C (400°F) Gas 6.

Spoon dollops of the mixture into the prepared moulds so that they do not quite fill them. Sprinkle with a little of the pearl sugar, if you have some.

Bake in the preheated oven for about 8–9 minutes until risen and golden. Tip onto a wire rack, then fill the mould with the remaining mixture and bake the second batch.

LINZERTORTE

150 g/1½ cups mixed finely ground hazelnuts and almonds

275 g/2 cups plain/all-purpose flour, plus extra to dust

1 teaspoon ground mixed spice/apple pie spice

½ teaspoon fine sea salt

225 g/1 cup cold unsalted butter, cut into cubes

85 g/½ cup plus 1⅔ tablespoons icing/confectioners' sugar

2 egg yolks, plus 1 egg yolk, beaten with a little water, to glaze

finely grated zest of 1 lemon and a squeeze of juice

3 tablespoons dry breadcrumbs

10 tablespoons each of redcurrant jelly and raspberry jam/jelly, mixed together

a 23-cm/9-in. fluted, round, loose-bottomed tart pan, greased

SERVES 10–12

Said to be the oldest cake in the world, this torte is named after the Austrian city of Linz. The crust is delightfully crumbly and its spiced, jammy filling is just the thing to take the edge off a wintry chill. A useful piece of advice to grind hazelnuts without them turning oily is to put them in a food processor with half the flour, and pulse them together until the hazelnuts are finely ground into the flour.

Preheat the oven to 180°C (350°F) Gas 4.

Mix the ground nuts, flour, mixed spice/apple pie spice and salt in a bowl. Add the butter and rub into the flour mixture with your fingertips until it resembles breadcrumbs. Add the icing/confectioners' sugar, stir well, then quickly mix in the two egg yolks, lemon zest and juice, so that the mixture starts to come together.

Turn out onto a lightly floured surface and knead briefly until smooth. Remove one-third of the dough. Shape the smaller piece into a disc, wrap in clingfilm/plastic wrap and chill in the fridge for 10 minutes.

Roll out the remaining dough on a lightly floured surface into a circle large enough to line the tart pan. Lift into the pan and press into an even layer over the base and sides, patching any gaps, as the dough is very crumbly. Add any trimmings to the pastry disc in the fridge. Chill the base for 10 minutes.

Put the base in the preheated oven and bake for 10–15 minutes until it has barely begun to colour, then set aside to cool. While the base is baking, roll out the remaining dough between 2 sheets of baking parchment into a circle about 25 cm/10 in., then return to the fridge for 20 minutes.

Sprinkle the cooked base of the torte with the breadcrumbs, then spoon the redcurrant jelly and raspberry jam/jelly evenly over the top (spoon on in blobs, and then use a palette knife/metal spatula to spread them out).

Remove the chilled pastry from the fridge and take off the sheets of baking parchment. Cut the pastry into strips, about 2 cm/¾ in. wide, across the diagonal. Lay these, one at a time, over the jam/jelly, using a long spatula, as the pastry is crumbly, to make a criss-cross lattice pattern. Neaten the edges by pressing any excess pastry against the side of the pan.

Brush the pastry with the egg yolk glaze, then bake for 45–50 minutes until golden. Allow to cool for 10 minutes before removing from the pan.

BEAVER TAILS

250 g/1¾ cups strong white bread flour

100 g/¾ cup self-raising/self-rising flour

50 g/heaping ⅓ cup strong wholemeal/whole-wheat flour

7 g/¼ oz sachet fast-action/rapid-rise dried yeast

1 teaspoon fine sea salt

1 teaspoon pure vanilla extract

200 ml/scant 1 cup whole/full-fat milk, just warmed

50 g/3½ tablespoons butter, melted and cooled

1 UK large/US extra-large egg

vegetable oil, to deep-fry

3 tablespoons caster/superfine sugar mixed with 1½ teaspoons ground cinnamon, to dust

MAKES 14

These are hand-stretched Canadian fried-dough pastries shaped like beaver tails. My recipe keeps things simple and serves them just with sugar and cinnamon, but in Canada they come with a wide range of toppings such as bananas and chocolate, whipped cream and crumbled cookies.

Mix the flours together in a bowl and add the yeast and salt to separate sides of the bowl. Mix the vanilla, milk, cooled melted butter and egg together, then add to the flour, mixing until you have a soft dough.

Turn the dough out onto a floured surface and knead for 10 minutes until smooth and supple. Put in a clean bowl, cover with a dishtowel, and leave to rise in a warm place for 1 hour, or until it has doubled in size.

Knock back/punch down the dough and divide it into 14 golf ball-sized pieces, about 50 g/2 oz. each. Roll and shape each one so that they are long and flat, like a beaver's tail, about 10 cm/4 in. long. Leave to rise, covered, for 10 minutes, then stretch them again to about 15 cm/6 in. long.

Heat about 5 cm/2 in. of oil in large wok or pan, large enough to hold a beaver tail. Once it reaches 170°C (340°F), drop in the dough pieces, a couple at a time, and cook, turning once or twice, for about 5–6 minutes until golden brown. Drain on paper towels, sprinkle with cinnamon sugar and serve.

BRIOCHE SAINT GENIX

15 g/½ oz. fresh yeast (or 7 g/¼ oz. sachet dried yeast)

175 ml/scant ¾ cup milk, warmed

350 g/2⅔ cups plain/all-purpose flour, plus extra to dust

2 eggs, plus 1 egg, beaten, to glaze

100 g/½ cup minus 1 tablespoon unsalted butter, softened

1 teaspoon salt

2 tablespoons caster/superfine sugar

200 g/7 oz. pink praline

50 g/2 oz. nibbed sugar

SERVES 6

The little pink pralines that are cooked inside and scattered on top of this brioche are what make it so special. The sugary praline dissolves into the dough giving it a distinct flavour and appearance. Track them down online at specialist sugarcraft suppliers.

Mix the yeast with a little of the warm milk and leave to froth for 10 minutes.

Put the flour in a bowl and add the remaining milk, the bubbly yeast, the two eggs, softened butter, salt and sugar. Mix to a soft dough then knead, in the bowl or in a mixer with a dough hook for 5–10 minutes until smooth and elastic. Cover with clingfilm/plastic wrap and leave to rise overnight in the fridge.

The next day, knead the dough on a lightly floured surface. Roll into a large square (about 50 cm/20 in.) and scatter with most of the praline. Fold each of the corners into the centre. Repeat this folding in of the corners twice more, until you have a neat dough square.

Put on the prepared baking sheet and cover with lightly greased clingfilm/plastic wrap. Leave for 1–2 hours until doubled in size.

Preheat the oven to 200°C (400°F) Gas 6.

Brush the top with the beaten egg to glaze and scatter with the remaining praline and the nibbed sugar.

Bake for 30 minutes until golden. Allow to cool on a wire rack before serving.

BRIOCHE

25 g/1 oz. fresh yeast (or 2 × 7 g/¼ oz. sachets dried yeast)

125 ml/½ cup lukewarm water

400 g/3 cups plain/all-purpose flour, plus extra for dusting

175 g/1¼ cups strong white bread flour

2 tablespoons caster/superfine sugar

2 teaspoons fine sea salt

4 eggs, plus 1 yolk, to glaze

125 ml/½ cup lukewarm milk

125 g/½ cup plus 1 tablespoon unsalted butter, diced and softened, plus extra, melted, to grease

12 individual 60-g/2-oz. brioche moulds

MAKES 12

I have a real fondness for brioche. They were one of the first things I ever learnt to bake when I was about six. Every Christmas we make a giant batch of brioche to eat warm at breakfast with extra butter and masses of maple syrup. The enriched dough is full of butter and eggs, so it also makes a fantastic teatime treat. Another little secret of a brioche dough is that it can be used in place of pastry for a beef Wellington or salmon en croûte.

Cream the fresh yeast with the water, or sprinkle the dried yeast over the surface of the water and leave to stand for 5 minutes until lightly frothy.

Mix the flours, sugar and salt in a large bowl and make a well in the centre. Beat the whole eggs into the warm milk, then pour into the well in the flour and add the yeast and water mixture. Mix well to form a soft dough.

Add half the diced butter to the dough and beat with a wooden spoon until smooth. At this point the dough is really soft. Dot the remaining butter over the surface of the dough, cover with a clean dishtowel and leave in a warm place for 1–2 hours until doubled in size.

Knock back/punch down the risen dough and then knead vigorously for 5 minutes. You want to make the dough really elastic, so pull and stretch it up and out of the bowl, then back down. When you can stretch it up to the height of your shoulder without it breaking, you have kneaded it enough.

Cover the bowl with lightly greased clingfilm/plastic wrap, put in the fridge and chill overnight.

The next day, brush the brioche moulds with melted butter. Turn the dough out onto a lightly floured surface and knead briefly until smooth. Weigh the dough, cut off one-quarter and set it aside. Divide the larger piece into 12, roll each piece into a ball and put in the buttered moulds. Divide the remaining dough into 12 and roll each into a small ball.

With scissors, cut a cross in the top of each of the larger dough balls in the moulds, then put a smaller ball on top. Put the moulds on a baking sheet, cover with a clean dishtowel and leave to rise for 30 minutes–1 hour until doubled in size.

Meanwhile, preheat the oven to 200°C (400°F) Gas 6.

Beat the egg yolk with a little water and use to brush the tops of the risen brioche. Bake in the preheated oven for 20 minutes until firm, well risen and golden. Turn out onto a wire rack to cool a little before serving.

BUGNES

500 g/3¾ cups plain/all-purpose flour, plus extra to dust

7 g/¼ oz. sachet fast-action/rapid-rise dried yeast

1 teaspoon fine sea salt

75 g/⅓ cup plus 1 tablespoon caster/superfine sugar

4 UK large/US extra-large eggs

2 tablespoons rum

85 g/⅓ cup plus 2 teaspoons unsalted butter, melted and cooled slightly

sunflower oil, to fry

caster/superfine sugar mixed with a little cinnamon, to dust

MAKES 60

These little fritters, or beignets, are a traditional part of Mardi Gras or 'Fat Tuesday', the day before the 40 days of Lenten fasting. (Pictured opposite.)

Put the flour into a bowl with the yeast, salt and sugar. Mix the eggs with the rum and melted butter. Make a well in the centre of the flour and pour in the wet mixture. Use a wooden spoon and then your hands to bring it together into a soft dough.

Knead in a stand mixer with a dough hook (or with your hands) for about 5–10 minutes until it is smooth and coming away from the side of the bowl. Cover and leave to rise for 2–3 hours or overnight in the fridge.

Heat a pan of oil over a medium heat until it reaches 180°C (350°F).

Dust the surface with flour and knock back/punch down the dough. Roll out the dough to 3 mm/⅛ in. thick.

Use a sharp knife to cut the dough into diamond shapes. Cut a small slit in the centre of each of the diamonds and pull one corner of the diamond through the hole. Or you can leave them with just the slit in the centre, or pull two ends through to make a sort of knot.

Cook the bugnes in batches, flipping halfway through, until golden. Drain on paper towels and sprinkle with sugar and cinnamon before serving.

RISSOLES SAVOYARDES

4 firm, just-ripe pears, peeled and cored

2 dessert apples, peeled and cored

20 g/1½ tablespoons unsalted butter, softened

50 g/¼ cup caster/superfine sugar

500 g/1 lb. 2 oz. all-butter puff pastry

plain/all-purpose flour, to dust

1 egg, beaten with a little milk

icing/confectioners' sugar, to serve

MAKES 12–16

These plump pastry slippers are filled with a soft and fragrant pear filling. Traditionally, the Blesson or Marlioz pear, which is from the Savoy region, was used. These are like quinces – tough and inedible until they are cooked, when they soften and become sweet. If you want to use quinces, poach them very slowly in half-and-half sugar and water until they are tender.

Preheat the oven to 180°C (350°F) Gas 4.

Slice the pears and apples, and layer them in a roasting pan. Dot all over with the butter, then sprinkle with the caster/superfine sugar.

Cover with foil and bake in the oven for 30 minutes. Remove the foil and bake for a further 30 minutes until caramelized. Set aside to cool completely.

Turn the oven up to 220°C (425°F) Gas 7.

Roll out the puff pastry on a floured surface to an even rectangle 3 mm/⅛ in.

thick, then cut it into strips 12 cm/4½ in. wide. Put heaped spoonfuls of the fruit along the length of one side of the pastry, about every 10 cm/4 in. Brush the edges with beaten egg and fold over, then cut into little parcels using a pizza wheel or pasta cutter to give a fluted edge (or you can use a sharp knife).

Put on a baking sheet and brush all over with the beaten egg. Bake for 15–20 minutes until golden and puffed. Leave to cool a little then serve dusted with icing/confectioners' sugar.

BAGUETTES

500 g/3½ cups strong white bread flour
350 ml/1½ cups water
7 g/¼ oz. sachet dried yeast
10 g/2 teaspoons fine sea salt
oil, to grease

baguette tray or a baking sheet and a stiff linen cloth

MAKES 3

Ask anyone what bread they most associate with France, and I'm sure they will say the baguette. The key to a top-notch baguette is to get a really crusty outside with a soft, but chewy, centre. The crust is created by the steam in your oven when you bake, and the centre is made using a simple yeast starter and allowing time for the dough to develop slowly.

Mix 120 g/¾ cup of the flour with 120 ml/½ cup water and one-third of the sachet of yeast to make a soft batter. Leave for 12 hours or overnight until bubbling. Add the remaining ingredients and mix to form a dough. Knead either in a mixer with a dough hook or by hand until you have a soft, smooth dough. It will start off quite sticky. If kneading by hand you will need to lift up the dough and slap it down onto the work surface, then fold and repeat.

Once smooth, put in a lightly oiled bowl, cover and leave to rise in a warm place for 3 hours. Every hour, very gently lift up the dough and turn it over, trying not to knock out all the air.

Gently turn out onto the work surface and divide into three equal pieces. Gently flatten each piece with your knuckles, rolling up at the same time into a smooth, longish shape. Cover with a dishtowel and leave to rest for 10 minutes.

Flatten each of the pre-rolled dough pieces into a rectangle about

23 cm/9 in. × 20 cm/8 in. Flip the long sides into the centre of the rectangle and press down gently. Flip the dough over onto the seam and then, with your hands, gently roll it into a baton shape.

Put the shaped baguettes onto a baguette tray or shape a stiff linen cloth into a rouched shape on a baking sheet and nestle the baguettes into it. Cover loosely and leave to rise for 30 minutes.

Preheat the oven to 220°C (425°F) Gas 7 and put in a baking sheet to heat up. Also put an empty small roasting pan on the bottom of the oven.

Using a sharp knife, make quick slashes along the axis of the loaves on a diagonal. If you have shaped them by hand, slide them carefully onto a floured baking sheet, and transfer them to the hot baking sheet using a sharp jiggle.

Pour a small amount of water into the hot roasting pan to create steam. Bake the baguettes in the preheated oven for 25–30 minutes until golden and risen with a lovely crust. Allow to cool before eating.

CROISSANTS

20 g/¾ oz. fresh yeast or 10 g/1 tablespoon fast-action/rapid-rise dried yeast

140 ml/generous ½ cup luke-warm water

500 g/3¾ cups plain/all-purpose flour, plus extra to dust

30 g/2½ tablespoons caster/superfine sugar

12 g/2 teaspoons fine sea salt

40 g/3 tablespoons unsalted butter, softened, plus 250 g/1 cup plus 2 tablespoons cold unsalted butter

140 ml/generous ½ cup luke-warm milk

1 egg, beaten with 1 tablespoon milk, to glaze

MAKES 12

One of the things I love most about our family ski trips are the croissants. Every morning my wonderful mum walks down the hill through the village to pick up our order of freshly made croissants and what we call 'bottom buns' (pains au lait, which are little buns with a cleft in the centre which, when we were small, made us giggle because they looked like buttocks, so the name stuck). We always order far more than we can eat at breakfast, because the most delicious thing is the joy of a cheese croissant after skiing. Think cheese on toast, but so much better. I couldn't think of writing a book about the food of the winter cabins without including a recipe for croissants. You might only make them for special occasions, but the sense of pride and achievement as you produce a home-made croissant is quite something. Just don't forget to make enough for a melty cheesy croissant later on!

Mix the yeast with 50 ml/scant ¼ cup of the warm water and set aside for 10 minutes. Put the flour in a bowl with the sugar, salt and the 40 g/3 tablespoons softened butter. Add the remaining water and the milk and the yeast mixture and bring together into a soft dough.

Knead with a dough hook in a stand mixer or by hand for a couple of minutes, but not too long, as you don't want the gluten to develop too much. Shape into a flat disc, wrap in clingfilm/plastic wrap and chill overnight.

Slice the cold butter into 1 cm/½ in. thick slices and lay on a sheet of baking parchment. Cover with another sheet of baking parchment and roll until you have a 20 cm/8 in. square. Trim to straighten the edges and put the trimmings on top, and then re-roll to make an 18 cm/7 in. square. Chill until needed.

Roll the dough into a 26 cm/10¼ in. square on a lightly floured surface. Put the chilled butter in the centre of the square at an angle so that it makes a diamond in the centre of the dough. Fold the corners of the dough up and over the butter into the centre.

Roll out the square gently until you have a rectangle about 20 × 60 cm/ 8 × 24 in. Keep it as even as possible. Take the top short side of the pastry and fold down into the centre, then fold the bottom up over the top, as you would fold a letter to put into an envelope. Cover and chill for 30 minutes then turn 90 degrees and roll and fold again. Repeat this process 3 times more, then chill overnight.

The next day, gently roll out the dough to a 20 × 110 cm/8 × 43 in. rectangle. Cut the dough into triangles by making diagonal cuts along the dough, one way then the other. Gently stretch each triangle out with the rolling pin. Roll up from the wide end of the triangle into croissant shapes, bringing the ends around to get the crescent shape. Put on a baking sheet and cover with clingfilm/ plastic wrap. Prove for 1–2 hours until doubled in size. Make sure they don't get too hot or the butter will melt out.

Preheat the oven to 200°C (400°F) Gas 6.

Brush the croissants with egg glaze and bake in the preheated oven for 18–20 minutes until golden and crisp.

PAIN AUX RAISINS

A truly wonderful breakfast treat, pain aux raisins have layers of light, buttery pastry filled with an almond filling and bursting with fruit. Dip them into cups of steaming black coffee for an authentically French breakfast. These are so easy to make at home, and they freeze really well, so you can eat half and freeze the rest for later.

20 g/¾ oz. fresh yeast

3 teaspoons caster/superfine sugar

110 ml/scant ½ cup milk, warmed

125 g/1 cup minus 1 tablespoon plain/all-purpose flour, plus extra to dust

125 g/¾ cup plus 2 tablespoons strong white bread flour

a good pinch of fine sea salt

1 egg, beaten

110 g/½ cup minus 1 tablespoon unsalted butter, softened

FOR THE FILLING

250 ml/generous 1 cup whole/full-fat milk

75 g/⅓ cup plus 1 tablespoon caster/superfine sugar

20 g/3 tablespoons plus 1 teaspoon cornflour/cornstarch

3 egg yolks

1 tablespoon pure vanilla extract

250 g/1¾ cups (dark) raisins

TO FINISH

1 egg, beaten

2 tablespoons caster/superfine sugar

baking sheet, lightly oiled

MAKES 15

Mix the yeast and 1 teaspoon of the sugar with a couple of tablespoons of the milk and leave for a few minutes until frothy. Put the remaining sugar, flours and salt in a bowl. Make a well in the centre and add the egg, warm milk and the yeast mixture. Stir together until you have a soft dough.

Knead on a lightly floured surface for 5 minutes, then flatten with your knuckles to a rough rectangle about 30 × 40 cm/12 × 16 in. Put on the oiled baking sheet and cover with clingfilm/plastic wrap. Chill for 30 minutes.

Slide the dough onto a lightly floured surface and dot the top two-thirds with softened butter, leaving a border around the edge. Fold the butter-free third up over, then the top third down to make a parcel. Press the edges together, then chill for 30 minutes.

Put the dough with a short side towards you and roll it out to a long rectangle, rolling in one direction, then, as before, fold the dough into thirds. Chill for 15 minutes, then repeat the process, but with a long side towards you. Repeat this rolling, folding and chilling process

until you have completed it 4 times. Wrap the dough in clingfilm/plastic wrap and chill overnight.

Make the filling. Heat the milk in a pan until almost boiling. In a bowl whisk the sugar, cornflour/cornstarch, egg yolks and vanilla. Pour over the hot milk and whisk until smooth. Pour back into the pan and cook over a medium heat, whisking constantly until very thick. Pour into a bowl and cover the surface with clingfilm/plastic wrap. Leave to cool, then chill.

Take the dough from the fridge, roll out to a 30 × 40 cm/12 × 16 in. rectangle and spread all over with the chilled filling. Scatter with the raisins. Roll up from the short side, then chill for 10 minutes. Slice into 15 slices and put, flat-side down, on a baking sheet. Chill for 20 minutes.

Preheat the oven to 200°C (400°F) Gas 6.

To finish, brush all over with beaten egg and bake for 18–20 minutes until golden.

Dissolve the caster/superfine sugar in 2 tablespoons water and bubble to a light syrup. Brush the warm buns all over with the glaze then cool and serve.

TRESSE

15 g/½ oz. fresh yeast (or 7 g/¼ oz. sachet fast-action/rapid-rise dried yeast)
240ml/1 cup whole/full-fat milk, warmed
500 g/3¾ cups plain/all-purpose flour
1¼ teaspoons fine sea salt
2 teaspoons honey
60 g/¼ cup unsalted butter, melted
1 egg, beaten, to glaze
oil, to grease

baking sheet, greased

MAKES 2

When I see beautiful, shining, golden tresse (also called a zopf in Austria) in a boulangerie, I just can't resist buying them. It's something about the way they pull apart along the lines of the braid that is so satisfying. They are crying out to be dunked into really good hot chocolate or smothered in butter and honey before a big day on the mountain.

Mix the yeast with 50 ml/scant ¼ cup of the warm milk and set aside. Put the flour and salt in a bowl, add the honey, butter, the remaining milk and the yeast mixture. Mix until you have a soft dough then turn out onto a lightly floured surface until smooth and elastic.

Put back into a clean bowl and cover with lightly greased clingfilm/plastic wrap. Leave in a warm place to double in size, this might take a couple of hours.

Divide into two and then split each half of dough into three even pieces. Roll out three of the pieces and pinch the tops together, then plait/braid the dough all the way down and press the ends together. Transfer to the prepared baking sheet and repeat with the other half of dough.

Cover with the clingfilm/plastic wrap again and leave to prove for 1 hour.

Preheat the oven to 180°C (350°F) Gas 4.

Brush the loaves with the egg to glaze and bake for 30 minutes until golden. Allow to cool a little then serve.

DRINKS AND HOT TODDIES

CHOCOLAT CHAUD

200 g/7 oz. dark/bittersweet chocolate, chopped

4 mugs of whole/full-fat milk (about 900 ml/generous 3¾ cups)

2 tablespoons caster/superfine sugar

4 tablespoons rum, kirsch or brandy (optional)

200 ml/scant 1 cup double/heavy cream

1 tablespoon icing/confectioners' sugar

SERVES 6

None of this powdered nonsense – a proper hot chocolate is made with pure chocolate melted into rich, creamy milk with a tot of something to warm the blood. (Opposite.)

Put the chocolate in a pan with the milk and the caster/superfine sugar. Heat very gently until the chocolate has dissolved. Add the booze, if you like, then pour into six mugs.

Whip the cream with the icing/confectioners' sugar then spoon onto the hot chocolate and serve immediately.

BOOZY COFFEE

450 ml/2 cups hot strong coffee

90 ml/⅓ cup plus 1 tablespoon Frangelico

25 ml/5 teaspoons kirsch

100 ml/scant ½ cup double/heavy cream

freshly grated nutmeg

MAKES 2

To round off the end of a glorious mountain meal.

Mix the coffee with the Frangelico and kirsch then whisk in 2 tablespoons of the cream and pour into two glasses.

Lightly whip the rest of the cream and dollop onto the coffee. Grate over a little nutmeg and serve.

HOT TODDY

140 ml/generous ½ cup water
140 ml/generous ½ cup whisky
finely grated zest of 1 lemon
2 teaspoons honey or caster/
superfine sugar
2 slices fresh ginger, peeled
2 cloves

MAKES 2

The classic hot toddy is not just a cure for colds and sniffles.

Put all the ingredients in a pan and heat together gently until the sugar or honey dissolves. Strain, pour into cups or glasses and serve.

GLÜHWEIN/VIN CHAUD

1 bottle full-bodied red wine
100 ml/scant ½ cup brandy
1 cinnamon stick
3 cloves
1 star anise
1 orange, sliced
1 lemon, sliced
50–75g/¼ cup–generous ⅓ cup caster/superfine sugar, to taste

SERVES 6–8

Wrapping your hands around a glass of steaming glühwein as you watch the snow fall is definitely one of the best things about mountain living. (Opposite.)

Put all the ingredients in a large pan with 250 ml/generous 1 cup water. Heat gently until the sugar dissolves, then serve ladled into mugs or glasses.

SPICED APPLE CIDER

600 ml/generous 2½ cups medium sweet cider
75 ml/scant ⅓ cup calvados or brandy
1 cinnamon stick
1 vanilla pod/bean, halved
a small knob/pat of butter

SERVES 4

Fruity and full of spices, you will find this slips down very easily.

Put the cider and calvados in a pan with the cinnamon and vanilla, heat gently until steaming then whisk in the butter and serve immediately.

KIR ROYAL

2 tablespoons crème de cassis
1 bottle sparkling wine or champagne

MAKES 6

The most classic of cocktails, fabulous as an aperitif. (Pictured opposite.)

Divide the cassis among 6 glasses then top up with champagne. It's one of the most simple yet delicious cocktails.

MAPLE OLD FASHIONED

60 ml/¼ cup bourbon whiskey
1 tablespoon maple syrup
a dash of bitters
a slice of orange

MAKES 1

An after-dinner sipper – the Canadian way.

Stir the bourbon with the maple syrup then add the bitters. Run the slice of orange around a rocks glass and fill with ice. Pour over the cocktail and add the slice of orange, and serve.

INDEX

ACKNOWLEDGMENTS

I truly love winter. The cosiness of the evenings as the day draws in, real fires, beautiful knitwear and snuggly slippers to keep out the chill. The hope and longing for snow, for days of cold, clear, crisp air and blue skies. Bracing walks and coming in from the cold. Most of all, I love the food. Rich, hearty pies and stews, creamy bakes and warming puds.

Writing a book on Alpine food is nothing short of a dream for me. So many of the dishes I have long enjoyed eating on ski trips and holidays in the mountains of Europe, but rarely cook for myself. It had been a true joy discovering how these dishes are made, and exploring recipes I have only ever heard of from other mountain fanatics.

I am so proud of this book, of its recipes and its beautiful pictures, which will hopefully inspire you to try these dishes for yourself.

One million thank yous to everyone who made this book as wonderful as it is. To my amazing sister Polly, whose styling, as ever, made everything look so fantabulous. Without her talent and superhuman effort and hours of support, this book just wouldn't be the same.

To my lovely Nass, whose pictures make this book so wonderful – working with you is a joy and a treat. Thank you for helping to eat everything and for coming all the way to the Alps in the search of snow and cabins to get the shots that have made all the difference. Also to Katrina, for reminding me that vegetarians need to eat too! Our vegetarian fondue bourguignon evening will go down in history and will definitely feature in another book!

Extra hugs and thanks to my fabulous assistant April, who rolled, kneaded, sautéed and baked alongside me, making sure everything was just so, I couldn't have done it without your help!

Thank you to Kate, Leslie, Toni, Julia and Cindy for believing in this book, for the hours spent making sure everything is just right and for listening and putting up with me! It has been so worth all the work to create this beautiful book.

To my amazing parents for loving the mountains and making them part of our lives. To my dadda who patiently took us up mountains and helped us down despite tantrums and tears, and my moomin mama, whose amazing cooking and love of feeding hungry skiers is where this all started.

Perhaps most importantly, thank you with my whole heart to the family Laurent for showing us the La Fouly way of life and letting us into your little slice of mountain heaven. It is as dear a place to me as any could be and is forever in my heart. Without you this book would certainly never have happened.